Interesting History of the Congo River

Compiled by

Emily Stehr

emilystehr@hotmail.com

Definition of Congo River

"Also called Zaire, a river in central Africa, flowing in a great loop from southeast Democratic Republic of the Congo to the Atlantic. About 3000 miles (4800 km) long.

"Congo – African nation, named for the river that runs through it, which is from a Bantu word meaning 'mountains' (ie, the river that flows from the mountains). As an adjective, *Congoese* is native English (1797) but has been supplanted by *Congolese* (1900), from French *Congolais*.

"Congo River – One of the world's longest rivers, it is Africa's largest potential source of electric power. Explored separately but simultaneously by the missionary David Livingstone and the journalist Henry Stanley, the Congo was the site of their proverbial encounter. (See 'Dr Livingstone, I presume?')"

http://www.dictionary.com/browse/congo--river

Ethiopia: I am the Congo River

By Getachew Robele

I am the rhythms; I am the bright face of the tropical rainforest
I flow into the sea of togetherness
My name is the flowing Gold, the flowing spirit: The Congo River

I am like the Amazon
I am like the Nile, I flow
Like the Ganges, like the Yangtze
Like the Mississippi, like Ohio, like the Danube, like the Rhine, like the Don
I flow into the sea of oneness
I end in the sea of greatness
I am the meeting of the life: Chambeshi, Ubangi, Sankuru, Kwango, Fimi, Kwa, Inkisi

I come from the highlands and mountains of myth
I was born after Bumba, the supreme God of creation,
Created what lives and dies in the world
Bumba who turned the eastward face of the mountains to westward
And made my journey like a walk on a carpet
I come from where the water spirit kuitikuiti reigned and ruled
Kuitikuiti he who married Mboze she who gave birth
To Bunzi the goddess of fertility
I am the son of Chambeshi and Lualaba
I am he who comes from Lapula from Uele from Sangha
When I run, I alternate my pace:
Now a slow pace, now a fast pace, now a slow pace, now a fast pace
Now zigzag, now a straight surge
Sometimes like a sprinter I run
Sometimes I jump
Sometimes I dive from hillsides and cliffs
And wash my face
With the white sprays of beauty

I run a long distance
I am a long distance runner

I am like the Amazon
My breath is the same: come together, flow together

While I run, the foam and ripples of the water is my smile
The song of the birds
The whispering of leaves the noise of my fans
The night stars and the moon and the sky: the spectators watching my pace
The passing clouds: the guests admiring from the sides

I sing, yes, I sing:

"If a dawn of truth meets you
Like an angle with good news
If the filtering in of the morning light
Of the sun through the trees, kisses you
Or stands and calls you to talk
That is the time to wake up
That is the time to greet the drum of hopes
That is the time to dance to the sounds of early birds of promise
That is the time to look at the sky's unveiled face
That is the time to listen to the echo of liveliness
That is the time to pick your hoes
And dig the soil, my children

"The rivers that hate to meet remain small rivers
They remain the thinning rivers
They remain the dying rivers on their way

"Whilst the face of the hills changes
Whilst the face of the mountains changes
The rivers that fail to change their course will cease to exist
Even the Amazon changed his course
From the westward to the eastward
Even the Mississippi changed his course
From the westward to the eastward
Even the Nile changed his course

"No one's course is a monument
No one's," I sing

I am the rhythms; I am the bright face of the tropical rainforest
I am the Congo River, that flowing Gold, that flowing spirit
Son of Chambeshi and Lualaba

11 September, 2009

TABLE OF CONTENTS

[YEAR OF PUBLICATION LISTED IN ASCENDING ORDER; PRIMARY AUTHOR LISTED ALPHABETICALLY FOR EACH YEAR]

1703: Dampier, William

1710: Tellez, Balthazar

1732: Churchill, Awnsham

1758: Postlethwayt, Malachy

1794: Wadstrom, Carl Bernhard

1797: Hawkins, Joseph

1817: Hulbert, Charles

1820: Strachan, James

1829: Howell, Esq John

1835: Priest, Josiah

1838: Wright, George Newenham

1840: Buxton, Sir Thomas Fowell

1840: Greg, William Rathbone

1840: MacQueen, James

1842: Bandinel, James

1843: Eldridge, Elleanor

1845: Tracy, Joseph

1847: Neilson, Peter

1848: Allen, W

1848: James (Rajah of Sarawak)

1848: Matson, Henry James

1849: Beke, Charles Tilstone

1849: Wilkes, Charles

1850: Appleyard, John Whittle

1851: Smith, John

1854: Cooley, William Desborough

1854: Maitland, James A

1855: Purdy, John

1857: Waterton, Charles

1858: Foster, John

1858: Stone, Elizabeth

1859: Great Britain

1860: Thomas, W

1861: American Anti-Slavery Society

1862: Stoddard, Elizabeth

1863: Hunt, James

1865: Christie, William Dougal

1869: Timbs, John

1871: Hawkey, Charlotte

1872: Burton, Sir Richard Francis

1873: The Lands of Cazembe

1874: Hoppin, James Mason

1874: Staden, Hans

1875: Jones, Charles H

1703: Dampier, William

William Dampier; A new voyage round the world. Vol 1 [of Dampier's voyages.]; 5th edition; James Knapton; 1703

William Dampier writes: "Our Chyrurgeon, Mr *Wafer,* came to a sad disaster here: being drying his Powder, a careless fellow palled by with his ripe lighted, and set fire to his Powder, which blew up and scorch'd his Knee; and reduced him to that condition, that he was not able to march; wherefore we allowed him a Slave to carry his things, being all of us the more concern'd at the accident, because lyable our selves every moment to misfortune, and none to look after us but him. This *Indian* Plantation was seated on the bank of the River *Congo,* in a very fat Soyl and thus far we might have come in our Canoa, if I could have perswaded them to it.

"The 6th day we set out again, having hired another guide. Here we, first crost the River *Congo* in a Canoa, having been from our first Landing on the West side of the River; and being over, we marched to the Eastward 2 mile, and came to another River, which we forded several times, though it was very deep. Two of our men were not able to keep company with us, but came after us as they were able. The last time we forded the River, it was so deep, that our tallest men stood in the deepest place, and handed the sick, weak, and short men; by which means we all got over safe, except those two who were behind. Foreseeing a necessity of wading through Rivers frequently in our Land-march, I took care before I left the Ship to provide my self a large Joint of Bambo, which I stopt at both ends, closing it with Wax, so as to keep out any Water. In this I preserved my Journal and other Writings from being wet, tho I was often forced to swim. When we were over this River we fat down to wait the coming of our Consorts who were left behind, and in half an hour they came. But the River by that time was so high, that they could not get over it, neither could we help them over, but bid them be of good comfort and stay till the River did fall, But we marched 2 mile farther by the side of the River, and there built our Hutts, having gone this day 6 miles. We had scarce finished our Hutts before the River rose much higher, and over-flowing the Banks, obliged us to remove into higher ground: But the next night came on before we could build more Hutts, so we lay straggling in the Woods, some under one Tree, some under another, as we could find convenience, which might have been indifferent comfortable if the weather had been fair, but the greatest part of the night we had extraordinary hard Rain, with much Lightening and terrible claps of Thunder. These hardships and inconveniences made us all careless, and there was no Watch kept, (tho I believe no body did sleep:) So our Slaves taking opportunity, went away in the nights all but one, who was hid in some hole and knew nothing of their design, or else fell asleep. Those that went away: carried with them our Chyrurgeons Gun and all his Money."

A new voyage round the world. Vol. 1 [of Dampier's voyages.].

1710: Tellez, Balthazar

Balthazar Tellez; The Travels of the Jesuits in Ethiopia; Vol 7 of A new coll of voyages and travels, and hist accout of discoveries; J Knapton; 1710

Balthazar Tellez writes: "Many were of Opinion, that the *Nile* had its Source in this Mercator Lake, which, as has Been said, only affords it a Passage; yet, tho' several others fall into it, none has any other Passage out of this Lake but that of the *Nile*; which shows, that *Mercator* and *Johnson* were both misform'd, when they say, that from this Lake flows the River Zaire, which after watering the Kingdom of *Congo* falls into the Western Ocean, and two other Rivers, which they pretend, meet in another Lake on the Borders of *Angola,* whence *Mercator* says, the River *Coanza* flows. However, molt certain it is, that only the *Nile* runs out of this Lake, and the *Coanza* has a far different Source."

The travels of the Jesuits in Ethiopia

1732: Churchill, Awnsham

Awnsham Churchill, Jean Barbot; A Collection of Voyages and Travels, Some Now First Printed from Original Manuscripts, Others Now First

Published in English: With a General Preface, Giving an Account of the Progress of Navigation, from Its First Beginning; Vol 1; Walthoe; 1732

Awnsham Churchill and Jean Barbot write: "*An* 1480. James Cam proceeded as far as the river Congo in the kingdom of the same name, called by the natives Zayre, whence he continued his voyage as far as 22 degrees of south-latitude, and thence home again."

Awnsham Churchill and Jean Barbot continue: "But let us return to speak farther of the river *Zaire*. This river is commonly said to take its rise in the kingdom of *Matamba,* subject to the queen of *Singa,* which kingdom being altogether governed by the female sex, I may number it among those nations described by *Claudian in Eutrop* lib I v 323.

"- *Medis, levibusque Sabaeis / Imperat bic sexus, reginarumq; sub armis / Barbariae pars magna jacet.*

"In this *Matamba* there is a vast collection of water, which dividing itself into two principal streams, one runs through *Ethiopia,* and in this river *Zaire,* and the other flows toward *Egypt,* being the *Nile:* This last was formerly adored by the *Egyptians* as a god, and that because of their being not able to find out its source, imagining that therefore it had none. I believe the cause why they could not discover its head, was by reason they could not go far up it, being hindered by the cataracts which fall in such a dreadful manner, that they at the same time offend both the eye and the ear. In this vast lake before mentioned before it divides it self into the aforesaid rivers, are to be found several water-monsters, amongst which there is one sort which differs from human kind only in want of reason and speech. Father *Francis da Pavia,* one of our missioners living in this country, would by no means believe that there were any such monsters in this lake, affirming they were only illusions devis'd by the *Negroes;* whereupon the queen of *Singa* being informed of his infidelity, invited him one day to go a fishing for them: Scarce had the fishermen thrown in their nets, but they discovered thirteen upon the surface of the water, whereof they could nevertheless take but one female, which was big with young. The colour of this fish was black, it had long black hair and large nails upon very long fingers, which perhaps were given it by nature to help its swimming: It lived not above twenty four hours out of the water, and during all that time would not taste any the least food that was offered it.

"Throughout all the river *Zaire* there is to be found the *mermaid*, which from the middle upwards has some resemblance of a woman, as in its breast, nipples, hands, and arms, but downwards it is altogether a fish, ending in a long tail forked: Its head is round, and face like to that of a calf: It has a large ugly mouth, little ears, and round full eyes: Upon its back it has a large hide tack'd, perforated in several places. This hide or skin seems to have been design'd by nature in a sort of manner to cover it, being contrived either to open or shut. The ribs of this fish are proper to stench blood, but the greatest of its physical virtues lies in two little bones in its ears. I have eat of this fish divers times, and it seems to be well-relished, and not unlike swines-flesh, which its entrails likewise resemble. For this reason the *Negroes* name it *ngullu a masa* (the water-sow) but the *Portuguese* call'd it *piexe molker* (the woman-fish.) Altho' it feeds on the herbs that grow on the sides of the river, yet does it not nevertheless ever go out of the water, but only hold its head out. For the most part it is to be taken only when it rains, for then the water being disturbed it cannot so well discern the approach of fishermen. Those that go to take them have a little boat for that purpose, in which they paddle up softly till the come to the place where the fish lies, and which they know by the motion it causes in the water; then having a lance ready, they immediately dart it with all their force into her, and if through the smallness of their boat, or for want of strength, they cannot hold her, they let go the lance and leave the fish at liberty, well knowing that being exceeding long the lance must necessarily discover where she flies with it. But if on the other hand they can maintain their stroke with another lance, they dart a second time, by which means at last they easily tire and take the fish. After the same manner, but with less trouble they take pilchards, which are fat, and as large as herrings, and they have no other way to take them but this. I should have told you what fort of fashioned lances these were, because they differ something from ours of *Europe;* they have a very long round staff made of wood, but as hard as iron, round, and so thick, that as many darts are made fast to it a small distance from one another, that they take up six or seven spans in compass."

Awnsham Churchill and Jean Barbot continue: "After this victory obtained, the aforesaid *calangola* proposed to the *Portuguese* captain to have all the prisoners killed, and given to his soldiers to eat, alledging that the *next day they should take as many more, and they would then not be able to keep both.* This proposal the captain either thro clemency or interest refused to consent to, telling the *Calangola,* that his men, if they pleased, might feed for the present on the dead bodies, and in the mean time he would consider of his request. Whilst this passed, the countess dowager, together with all the people, petition'd the said captain, *That he would proceed no further with his hostilities, and he should be fully satisfied in what he demanded.* To which the captain answered, *That he was resolved to go on as far as the farthest* banza [Banza *is a name given to the cities here.*], *to teach the* Sognese *people the bounds of their obedience to* Congo. Hereat the people being extremely enraged, one of the principal among them being of the blood of the counts, stood up, and told them, *That if they would elect him for their count, he would soon rid them of their fears of the* Portugueses. To this the affrighted people immediately consented, and at the same time chose him for their sovereign. Being thus chosen, he began to unite and fortify the distracted minds of his subjects; and to the end they might quickly be in a condition to take the field, he gave them the following instructions. First he order'd them to shave their heads (which custom continues even to this day among these people, whether males or females.) Next he commanded them to bind palm-leaves about their temples, to the end that in the battle they might be thereby distinguished from those *Blacks* that accompanied the *Portugueses.* He further advised them not to be afraid either of the noise or flashings of guns, since they were only as bugbears fit to fright children, and not men of courage. He moreover cautioned them against minding those *European* trifles which their enemies the *Whites* were accustomed to throw among them, when they had a mind to disorder and make them break their ranks. He likewise ordered them to shoot always at the men, and not the horses, these last being inconsiderable in war, and nothing like to the nature of tygers, lions and elephants. He commanded them moreover that if any among them turn'd his back, they should immediately strike off his head; and if more than one did the same, the rest should serve him the like: "*For* (says he) *we are all resolved to die a glorious death, rather than live a miserable life.* Lastly, to the end that his followers might go on under him with the less concern, he commanded them to kill all their domestick animals; and the better to encourage them therein, was the first that set them an example, by killing his own in their sight. This he did likewise to prevent the *Portugueses* (in case they should have the better of him) from having any thing to triumph over, and feast with in his dominions; and rather chose to have his subjects feed on them, to hearten and strengthen them for battle, than to have his enemies fatten and regale on his spoils. Now because his orders had been so punctually observed in this particular, the whole race of these beasts, especially of cows, has almost been totally destroyed ever since; insomuch that I my self have known a young maid sold here for a calf, and a woman for a cow. To reinforce this his army, the last thing this count did was to call in his neighbours to his assistance, together with whom and his own subjects having composed a wondrous force, he forthwith march'd out into the field. His enemies through too great a negligence and contempt of his power, soon betrayed themselves into his hands; for marching on without the least order, they gave opportunity to an ambush that lay ready for them, to break, and put them easily to flight. The first that fled were the *Giaghi,* being the troops under the *calangola,* and the forces of the king of *Congo* followed soon after. The slaves that had been taken in the battle before, finding here an opportunity to escape, run like madmen in amongst their friends, and having their arms unloosed by them, presently turn'd all their fury upon the remaining *Portugueses,* who still kept their ground; but at length being overpower'd by numbers, they were forced to give back, and were all kill'd in the pursuit, except six who were taken prisoners, and brought before the count; who demanded of them, *If they would chuse to die with their companions, or survive to he made slaves?* To which they answer'd, with an accustom'd *Spanish* resolution, *Never did* Whites *yet yield to he made slaves to* Blacks, *neither would they.* Which answer soon caused their destruction, for scarce were the words out of their mouths, but they were all killed upon the spot. All the artillery and baggage was taken by the *Sognese* army; the former of which, together with some pieces of cannon bought of the *Hollanders,* served to furnish a fortress built with earth at the mouth of the river *Zaire,* which commands both the said river and the sea.

"Before they left *Loanda,* the *Portuguese* army had desired of the commander of the *Armadilia* (so they call'd their fleet by reason of the smallness of it) *that as he sail'd along the coasts* of Sogno, *where-ever he saw great fires burning he should anchor.* Now after the obtained victory, the *Sognese* soldiers spent all their nights in jollity and merriment about such fires, as had been described; which the ships immediately perceiving, dropt their anchors hard by, and were preparing to land their force; while discovering from the shore a *Portuguese* slave that hal'd them, they soon took him into a boat, and found he had been sent by the count to the governor of *Loanda* with a leg and an arm of a *White;* together with this insulting message, *Go carry the news of your defeat, together with this present, to the governor of* Loanda *your master.* Thus you may perceive the seamen, if they had landed, had been in the same case with the landmen, and instead of imprisoning the *Blacks* in the shackles they had carried along with them for that purpose, had been undoubtedly in the like condition themselves, and had been at least made slaves of, if they came off with their lives.

"What the *Sognese* say for themselves in justification of this quarrel, is as follows: They ask first, *What right the king of* Congo *had to give away their country of* Sogno *to the* Portugueses, *when it was none of his, but a sovereignty of it self?* And next they would know, *Why the* Portugueses, *who were not unacquainted with that particular, should be so unjust as to be ready to accept of it, and that in an hostile manner?* They alledg'd moreover, *That when the* Hollanders *some years since had got possession of the kingdom of* Angola, *a great number of* Portugueses *being outed thence, fled to* Sogno, *where they were courteously entertained by the count, who gave them the island of* Horses *to live in; and moreover furnished them with all manner of provisions* gratis. *Now they could not but much wonder that those people whom they had so hospitably relieved, should have the ingratitude to endeavour to take their country away from them.* These jars arising upon this occasion, could not but be extremely prejudicial to the infant growth of Christianity in this country, insomuch that one of our order who lived at *Sogno* died for mere grief thereof: And I my self met with several people in *Chitombo,* the place where the battle was fought, who would come no more to confession upon that account.

"Now to return to our story: The count having received in the aforesaid battle about thirteen wounds, in near the compass of a month, died thereof; and a new one being soon chosen in his stead, he nourished in his heart so great a hatred to the *Portugueses,* that he resolved for the future to have no more dealings neither with them nor the *Capuchins,* whom he looked upon to belong to them. Whereupon sending for some *Flemish* merchants that were just then upon their departure out of his country for *Flanders,* he writ by them to the pope's nuncio there, to furnish his dominion with new priests. The pious prelate upon the receipt of this letter, sent him two *Franciscans* and one lay-brother, with strict command to them, that if there were any *Capuchins* in the country, they should submit to them as their superiors. These three religious persons being arrived, were received with all the courtesy imaginable, and afterwards conducted to our convent. The count perceiving that he had now got other priests, made use of several false pretexts no send ours away; and at last being not able to prove any crimes against them, he had recourse to the most barbarous and arbitrary usage that could be thought on, commanding that they should be dragged out of his dominions for the space of two miles together. This was forthwith executed with the greatest rigour, for the officers of this cruel master, not only tore them along in their own cords, with their faces grating downwards upon the sands, but likewise revil'd them all the way with unmerited reproaches and calumnies. All which notwithstanding these pious fathers underwent with the greatest chearfulness, well remembring what greater punishments and indignities their Saviour had suffered for them before. So great nevertheless were the injuries offer'd to these fathers, that in no long time after one of them died; and the other, who was the aforesaid father *Thomas,* hardly escaped with his life. Being thus misused, and withal unprovided of all necessaries, they were at last left on the confines of the count's dominions, in a little uninhabited island of the river *Zaire.* Here they made shift to support themselves for two or three days; F *Thomas,* who was the least hurt of the two, going out to hunt for their subsistence: but at length they were unexpectedly delivered from hence by some pagan fishermen, who took them on board them, and carried them to a city of their's called *Bombangoij* in the kingdom of *Angoij.* Here arriving at night, they were very courteously entertained by an infidel of the place, who gave them a supper, and moreover assigned them a house, and three women to wait on them after the manner of that country. But our fathers not caring to trust themselves among these people, soon after they had supp'd, sending away their women, meditated an escape. For this purpose father *Thomas,* who was the best able to walk, took his lame companion upon his back, and marched out of the house; but he had not gone far, but he was forced, through weakness, to set down his burden under a great shady tree; which as soon as day appeared, for fear of discovery, they made shift to get up into. Their patron coming that morning to visit his guests, and finding them gone, much wondered; and well knowing they could not be got far, by reason of the condition he left them in, immediately went about to search after them. Coming at last near the place where they were, and not having yet found them, a pagan thought came into his head that they might have been carry'd away by some spirits, and which he express'd after this manner; *If the devil has carried them away, I suppose he did it that they might make me no recompense for my kindness.* Our fathers hearing this, could not forbear laughing, even amidst their miseries and misfortunes, and putting out their heads from the tree, cry'd out, *We are here, friend, never doubt our gratitude, for we only went out of the house to refresh our selves with the rays of the rising sun.* Hereat the old man being exceedingly rejoiced, immediately took them down, and putting them into two nets, sent them away to *Capinda,* a port of the kingdom of *Angoij,* about two days journey from *Bombangoij.* Here, if I am not mistaken, the father that had been most harass'd, died; and father *Thomas* embarking himself not long after, on board a vessel that lay there, departed from *Loanda* in the kingdom of *Angola.* One of the two *Franciscans* that remained yet in *Sogno,* the other having been gone for Angola some time before, being extremely affronted at the ill usage of these two *Capuchins,* signified to the count that he thought himself obliged in charity to go in quest of his banished brethren, and that either to support them if alive, or bury them if dead. This request the count highly approved of, and consequently gave him leave to go. Having hereby obtained his desire, he soon set out for *Capinda,* but never returned, thinking it rather adviseable to go on board the same vessel with father *Thomas* for *Loanda.*

"His companion the lay-brother not finding him to return, obtained leave likewise to go on the same errand, as well as under pretence of hastening his return; but being once out of sight, he also was no more to be seen. Our convent thus being deprived of all its inhabitants, only one lay-brother remaining behind, whom the count kept locked up for fear of losing him; the people rose in great fury against their prince, and that for depriving them of the mission designed for their good. No prudence being capable of opposing this mutiny, they at last went so far that they seized upon their count, and sent him bound to an island of his dominions in the *Zaire;* where, that he might not be absolutely idle, they left him liberty to command, and afterwards chose a new count. This prince being but little satisfied with his confinement, did all that in him lay to get himself restored, intriguing incessantly with the neighbouring nations for that purpose. But which coming timely to his subjects ears, they once more seized upon him, and trying a huge weight to his neck, threw him in a rage into the sea, with these words; *Over this river you made the poor innocent* Capuchins *to pass into banishment for no offence, and into the same go you barbarous and inhuman monster, for so doing.* Thus ended the life of a persecutor of poor harmless men, who offended him only in that they were either really, or else suspected to be *Portugueses.*

"Whilst matters went thus, father *Joseph Maria,* who lived then at *Loanda,* after some time came to *Sogno,* under pretence of carrying away the lay-brother beforementioned, with some church-utenils belong to the mission, though in reality his business was to sound the minds of the *Sognese* people. After his arrive at the mouth of the river *Zaire,* called by the *Portugueses Pionta del Padron,* before he would set foot ashore, he sent a messenger to acquaint the count with his being there. As soon as the people heard of it, they hurried away in great numbers to see him, and presently acquainted him *how they had dispatched the enemy of the* Capuchins *into that river, and that for the future they would defend those holy men to the last drop of their blood.* This promise that afterwards confirmed by an oath at the holy altar. They also at the same time earnestly entreated this father, *that he would continue among them, and depart no more for* Loanda. To this request father *Joseph* answered, *That his commission from his superior extended no farther than to bring away father* Leonard, *together with the church goods.* In short, so very urgent were their intreaties, and so powerful their reasons, that he was at length prevailed upon to tarry with them; and that especially at the return of the messenger who brought him the same desires from the new count. All this gained so far upon him, that he not only consented to stay himself, but likewise, as a farther token of good-will, and pardoning their late offence, procured also the injured father *Thomas* to return once more among them; and even from thence forward our order has lived in that country without the least molestation."

Awnsham Churchill and Jean Barbot continue: "Being thus got into the spacious fields of *Sogno,* let us take a view by the by of the situations, possessions, habitations and manner of living, and clothing of those *Ethiopians.* The earldom of *Sogno* is absolute, except only its being tributary to the kingdom of *Congo.* It is a *peninsula,* bordering on the east upon *Bamba,* a dutchy belonging to *Congo,* and divided from it by the river *Ambrise:* on the west and south it has the ocean, and on the north it is bounded by the river *Zaire,* which divides the Christians from the pagans of the kingdom of *Angoli,* and is seated in the torrid zone, being only six degrees distant from the equinoctial line. It has several islands in the *Zaire,* which are all inhabited by Christians. The election of the count is performed by nine electors, who for the most part chuse a new one before the old one deceased is buried. During the interim of the *sede vacante* (vacancy of the throne) a child governs, who is obey'd by all as if he were their real prince. As soon as the election is made, we missioners are acquainted with it by order, to the end that if we approve of it we may publish it in the church, otherwise the election goes for nothing."

A Collection of Voyages and Travels, Some Now First Printed from Original Manuscripts, Others Now First Published in English: With a General Preface, ...

1758: Postlethwayt, Malachy

Malachy Postlethwayt; The importance of the African expedition considered; 1758

Malachy Postlethwayt writes: "The river *Congo* or *Zaira is* the most considerable in this part. On it's banks the *Portuguese* have established their government; and here resides in a spacious palace, their viceroy with great magnificence, at St *Salvadore,* or the city of *Congo.* The palace itself is said to contain three churches; and in the city they have twelve churches and seven chapels, besides the cathedral; which, it is said, is very capacious, plain without, but extravagantly rich and splendid within. There are also several monasteries of religious."

The importance of the African expedition considered

1794: Wadstrom, Carl Bernhard

Carl Bernhard Wadstrom; An essay on colonization, particularly applied to the Western coast of Africa, with some free thoughts on cultivation and commerce, also brief descriptions of the colonies already formed, or attempted … in Africa, including those of Sierra Leone and Bulama; 1794

Carl Bernhard Wadstrom writes: "76. As an instance, in support of this position, the doctor mentions the Portuguese town of St Salvadore, which, 'notwithstanding it lies 150 miles up the river Congo, or Zaire, and within six degrees of the equator; yet, from it's being situated on a hill, and the neighbouring country being cleared of the natural woods and thickets, it's inhabitants breathe a temperate and pure air, and are in a great measure, exempted from all the plagues of an unhealthy climate.'"

Carl Bernhard Wadstrom continues: "204. In 1484, Congo was discovered by Diego Cam, who, in behalf of his sovereign, King John of Portugal, formed an alliance, with the King of Congo, which has continued to the present day, with some interruptions, on the part of the Portuguese. Their chief town, St Salvadore, is situated 150 miles up the river Congo, or Zaire, upon an eminence, in a country well cultivated and most uncommonly salubrious. It is a very extensive place, but not proportionably populous, as the houses are intermixed with spacious gardens, which, doubtless, is one cause of it's salubrity. Yet it's inhabitants must be very numerous, as it is said to have twelve churches and seven chapels, besides the cathedral."

An essay on colonization, particularly applied to the Western coast of Africa, with some free thoughts on

cultivation and commerce; also brief descriptions of ...

1797: Hawkins, Joseph

Joseph Hawkins; A History of a Voyage to the Coast of Africa: And Travels Into the Interior of that Country: Containing Particular Descriptions of the Climate and Inhabitants, and Interesting Particulars Concerning the Slave Trade; 2nd edition; 1797

Joseph Hawkins writes: "The course that we had hitherto pursued was tedious, and though not destitute of pleasures, was fatiguing, and attended with danger. We had calculated the distance we had come as well as we could, and concluded that we must be not far from the LITTLE CONGO river; we determined to follow the course of the ravine, to the place into which the water discharges itself; often were we on the verge of retracing the path we had come up to the summit, the fatigue was so excessive, and the heat which reflected from the rocks and a chalky loam on the sides of the ravine became intolerable; it became necessary to take up our nights rest in this glen, where we rested well, but with our fires as usual."

A History of a Voyage to the Coast of Africa: And Travels Into the Interior of that Country: Containing Particular Descriptions of the Climate and Inhabitants, and ...

1817: Hulbert, Charles

Charles Hulbert; The African traveller; or, Select lives, voyages, and travels; Nineteenth Century Collections Online: Mapping the World: Maps and Travel Literature; 1817

Charles Hulbert writes: *"Total failure of the Expedition up the River Congo.*

"THE detailed accounts of the expedition to explore the Congo, or Zaire, have reached the Admiralty. Melancholy as the result has been, from the great mortality of the officers and men, owing to excessive fatigue, rather than to the effects of climate, the journals of Captain Tuckey and the gentlemen in the scientific departments are, it is said, highly interesting and satisfactory, as far as they go; and we believe they extend considerably beyond the first Rapid or Cataract. It would seem, indeed, that the mortality was entirely owing to the land-journey beyond these Rapids - and that Captain Tuckey died of complete exhaustion, after leaving the river, and not from fever. The climate, we understand, was remarkably fine; scarcely a shower of rain, or any humidity in the atmosphere, and the sun seldom shining out but for a few hours in the middle of the day; Farenheit's thermometer seldom exceeding 76 degrees by day, and never descending below 60 degrees at night - such a climate, in fact, as one would wish to live in; but an anxious zeal and over eagerness to accomplish the objects of the expedition, and to acquire all the information that could possibly be obtained, seem to have actuated every one, from the lamented commander to the common seaman and private marine, and led them to attempt more than the constitution was able to bear. The total number of deaths amount to 18; of which 14 were on the land expedition. They consist of Captain Tuckey, commander of the expedition; Lieutenant Hawkey, lieutenant of the Congo; Mr Professor Smith, botanist; Mr Tudor, comparative anatomist; Mr Cranch, collector of objects of natural history; Mr Galwey, a friend of Capt Tuckey, who volunteered from pure love of science; Mr Eyre, the purser. The names of the remainder have not been returned. The Dorothy transport, that accompanied the Congo into the river, lost but one man, and he fell overboard and was drowned. The following extract of a letter from Mr Mackerrow, the surgeon of the Congo, details some of the melancholy particulars of the symptoms which the sufferers exhibited previous to their death: -

"'Of the eighteen who died in the river, fourteen had been on shore, marching for some time, and were far advanced before reaching the ship. Professor Smith, who saw many of them when ill, gave to some a dose of calomel, but to others nothing had been administered. The fever appeared in some degree contagious, as all attendants upon the sick were attacked; and before we left the river, it pervaded nearly the whole crew; also some of the transports; but us for myself, although constantly among them, I did not feel the slightest indisposition until we left the coast when I was attacked; however, I considered mental anxiety, and disturbed rest, as the sole causes. Captain Tuckey had been afflicted many years with a chronic *hepatitis;* and on returning from travelling five weeks on shore, he was so excessively reduced, that all attempts to restore the energy of his system proved ineffectual. Mr Tudor was in the last stage of fever before I saw him; as were Messrs Cranch and Galwey. Professor Smith died in two days after he came under my care; during which time he refused every thing, whether as nutriment or medicine. Lieutenant Hawkey was taken ill after leaving the river, and died on the fourth day: his case was rather singular – the symptoms were, irritability of stomach, with extreme languor and debility; but he had neither pain nor fever. Mr Eyre had a violent fever, and on the third day breathed his last: before death, a yellow suffusion had taken place, with vomiting of matter resembling coffee grounds.'

"Extract of a Letter from Bahia, Oct 30. – 'We are enabled to give you a piece of intelligence, which will to many be of great interest – we mean the failure of the Expedition sent out by your Government early in the year 1816, under the command of Capt Tuckey, whose object was to explore the river Congo. Like all former enterprises of a similar kind, and notwithstanding the presumed discernment and skill of those concerned in the planning and executing of it, there appears to have been a want of foresight, both as to the time and means. However, as, no doubt, publicity will in due time be given to all their proceedings, it will suffice for us to acquaint you, that yesterday arrived in this port, his Majesty's ship Congo, and the Dorothy transport, from Cabenda, in 28 days, under the command of Mr Fitzmaurice, formerly master, but who succeeded in consequence of the death of Captain Tuckey and the Lieutenant, both of whom died at sea, the former on the 3rd, and the latter of the 5th instant. It appears, that they arrived at the mouth of the Congo about the 3d of July; and leaving the transport, which only accompanied them at an inconsiderable distance, they proceeded in the sloop, which was built purposely to draw little water, up the river, to the extent of 120 miles; when her progress, and even that of their boats, was stopped in insuperable difficulties; principally, we believe, by the rapids, which they express as beyond all description. Determining still on the further prosecution of their undertaking, the men were landed; and it was not until they had marched 150 miles (and 120 more than any white person had been before) over a barren and exceedingly mountainous country, after experiencing the greatest privations from the want of water, and being entirely exhausted by fatigue, that they gave up the attempt. Hope induced the most of them to traverse their route, and regain the vessel; but, alas! nature had been completely worn out; for most of them, say 25 out of 55, died 24 hours after their return, comprehending all the scientific part of the Europeans; and, we believe, only eight on board are now in a state to work the vessel; but as their chief want seems to be nourishment, it is to be hoped the others will soon be brought round. Suspicions are entertained, that many died by poison, administered by the natives; and Mr Fitzmaurice says, that he is persuaded that he could penetrate an immense way into the country without apprehending danger from any other cause, as the people are very pusillanimous, and easily intimidated. As a matter of courtesy and expediency, they asked permission of the Kings to pass their respective territories, which was generally readily granted; as the same time, they were furnished with plenty of natives as guides, at a moderate charge; but latterly advantage was taken of their difficulties. Mr Fitzmaurice and the surgeon are determined on a new attempt, if the Admiralty will fit out another expedition; and as he thinks he can provide against all casualties, he has great hopes of attaining the desired end.' – *Gent Mag. Feb* 1817."

The African traveller; or, Select lives, voyages, and travels

1820: Strachan, James

James Strachan, Joseph Brant; A visit to the province of Upper Canada, in 1819; printed by D Chalmers & co for J Strachan; 1820

James Strachan and Joseph Brant write: "Let four north-west canoes be brought to England, with picked crews of twelve men each; let them be put on board a vessel, and transported to the mouth of the river Zaire. These canoes carry twenty men each, with provisions and necessaries for four months. The provisions to consist of pemican, which can be packed in the usual manner. The men belonging to each canoe under regular officers, of determined resolution; and the whole under one commander. Every person, capable, on an emergency, of using his arms. A sufficient stock of presents for the natives would not occupy which room, as they might consist of such shewy articles as attract the notice of barbarians."

A Visit to the Province of Upper Canada, in 1819

1829: Howell, Esq John

Esq John Howell (of Edinburgh); The Life and Adventures of Alexander Selkirk Containing the Real Incidents upon the Romance of Robinson Crusoe is Founded. ... With an Appendix, Etc; 1829

Esq John Howell writes: "Just as the two launches entered the river of Santa Maria, to proceed towards the town, which lies upon the north side, about three leagues up the stream, a canoe with three Indians came in sight from the Congo river. The English not having been seen by them, put in behind a point of land near the junction of the currents, and took them before they were aware. As it was getting towards evening, Stradling removed one of the Indians into his launch, and sent the others, with five men in the canoe, to ascertain the position of Schucadero on the left side, as Dampier had directed. As it soon became quite dark, they could not find it; but, hearing a multitude of dogs barking on the south side, they concluded there must be a town. They stood over, when, just as they reached the shore, the two Indians leaped overboard, and they saw no more of them. One of the men fired after them, the report of whose piece was answered by a gun from the bank. A volley was then given; after which they landed, advanced to the town, and took it without resistance. The inhabitants fled at the first alarm, having been put on their guard by the five Indians who escaped at the mouth of the river."

The Life and Adventures of Alexander Selkirk Containing the Real Incidents Upon which the Romance of Robinson Crusoe is Founded.... With an Appendix, …

1835: Priest, Josiah

Josiah Priest; The Wonders of Nature and Providence, Displayed: Compiled from Authentic Sources, Both Ancient and Modern, Giving an Account of Various and Strange Phenomena Existing in Nature, of Travels, Adventures, Singular Providences, etc; 1835

Josiah Priest writes: *"An account of the wonderful deliverance of a sailor from the jaws of a tyger and an alligator in the river Congo.*

"SOME time after my arrival at the British factory, Cape Casta, on board the Davenport Guineaman, I was sent for by the commodore, who was stationed in the Diana frigate to protect the trade of the place before mentioned, and appointed by him to command a sloop, employed on the service of conveying slaves, teeth, gums, and other merchandize, from the company's factories, situated several hundred miles up the river Congo, down to the principal depot at the Cape. The sloop carried six swivels, and was manned with nine negroes, and two north countrymen, named Johnson and Campbell, the former of whom was my mate.

"After receiving orders relative to the duty in which I was employed, we proceeded on our voyage, and had navigated near fifty leagues up the country, when one morning the breezes died away suddenly, and we were compelled, by a strong current running against us, to drop anchor within a quarter of a mile of the shore. In this situation the sloop remained for three days, during which time, the circumstances fell out I am about to communicate; circumstances so improbable in themselves, so marvellous, as almost to border upon impossibility, but nevertheless, declared by me, as a spectator, to be the most perfect reality.

"To resume my narrative: - the bosom of the deep appeared, as it does in those parts while the calm prevails, extremely tranquil, and the heat, which was intolerable, had made us so languid, that almost a general wish overcame us, on the approach of the evening, to bathe in the waters of Congo: however, myself and Johnson were deterred from it, from the apprehension of sharks, many of which we had observed in the progress of our voyage, and those enormously large. At length Campbell alone, who had been making too free with his liquor case, was obstinately bent on going overboard; and although we used every mean in our power to persude him to the contrary, he dashed into the watery element, and had swam some distance from the vessel, when we, on the deck, discovered an alligator making towards him from behind a rock that stood a short distance from the shore. His escape I now considered impossible, his destruction inevitable, and I applied to Johnson how we should act, who, like myself, affirmed the impossibility to save him, and instantly seized a loaded carbine to shoot the poor fellow, before he fell into the jaws of the monster. I did not, however, consent to this, but waited with horror the tragedy we anticipated; yet willing to do all in my power, I ordered the boat to be hoisted, and we fired two shot at the approaching alligator, but without effect, for they glided over his scaly covering like hail-stones on a tiled penthouse, and the progress of the creature was by no means impeded. The report of the piece, and the noise of the blacks in the sloop, made Campbell acquainted with his danger, he saw the creature making for him, and with all the strength and skill he was master of, made to the shore. And now the moment arrived, in which a scene was exhibited beyond the power of my humble pen perfectly to describe. On approaching within a very short distance of some canes and shrubs that covered the bank, while closely pursued by the alligator, a fierce and furious tyger sprang towards him, at the instant the jaws of his first enemy were extended to devour him. At this awful moment Campbell was preserved. The eager tyger, by overleaping him, encountered the gripe of the amphibious monster. A conflict ensued between them - the water was covered with the blood of the tyger, whose efforts to tear the scaly covering of the alligator were unavailing; while the latter had also the advantage of keeping his adversary under water, by which the victory was presently obtained, for the tyger's death was now effected. They both sank to the bottom, and we saw no more of the alligator. Campbell was recovered, and instantly conveyed on board; he spoke not while in the boat, though his danger had perfectly sobered him, and what is more singular, from that moment to the time I am writing, he has never been seen the least intoxicated, nor has he been heard to utter a single oath. If ever there was a perfectly reformed being in the univere, Campbell is the man.'"

The Wonders of Nature and Providence, Displayed: Compiled from Authentic Sources, Both Ancient and Modern, Giving an Account of Various and Strange ...

1838: Wright, George Newenham

George Newenham Wright; A New and Comprehensive Gazetteer; Vol 5; T Kelly; 1838

George Newenham Wright writes: "The Portuguese, by their military exploits and the fame of their maritime discoveries, began, about the commencement of the 15th century, to attract the notice of other European states. The coast of Africa, as far south as Cape Nun or Non, Latitude 28 39 North, had been repeatedly explored; but, beyond that, nothing was known. Assisted, however, by the mariner's compass, which had lately been brought into use, these intrepid navigators discovered, in 1420, the island of Madeira. In 1433, Cape Nun was doubled for the first time, by Gillionez; and, about the same time, the Azores were discovered. By slow but progressive movements the Portuguese reached Senegal (1445), and eleven years afterwards discovered the Cape de Verd Islands. Next, Pierre de Cintra ventured as far as Cape Mesurada, on the Grain Coast, Latitude 6 18 North, where the land, stretching towards the east, seemed to promise a speedy accomplishment of their wishes, namely, a circumnavigation of the African continent. Prince's Island, Annabona, and St Thomas's were discovered by the Portuguese voyagers in 1471; the river Zaire, in Congo, was entered by Diego Cam, in 1484; and, two years after, Bartholomew Diaz reached the Cape of Good Hope. Vasco de Gama, having doubled the Cape in 1497, visited Port Natal, Mozambique, and Melinda, and, after traversing the Arabian Sea, he landed, in 1498, at Calicut, on the Malabar coast, the greater part of which he soon after explored. The whole eastern coast of Africa was examined, and the island of Ceylon discovered, about the year 1506. Five years after, the Portuguese established themselves at Malacca; and their discoveries after this period were so numerous and so rapid that, before the conclusion of 1520, they had visited and named most of the groups of islands on the Southeast and East of Asia, as far as Latitude 30 0 North."

A New and Comprehensive Gazetteer

1840: Buxton, Sir Thomas Fowell

Sir Thomas Fowell Buxton; The African Slave Trade, and Its Remedy; J Murray; 1840

Sir Thomas Fowell Buxton writes: "Commodore Owen shortly afterwards (in 1827) visited Kassenda, near the river Congo, which place, he says, 'is principally resorted to by slavers, of whom five were at anchor, in the harbor, on our arrival, one French, and the rest under the Brazilian flag.'"

The African Slave Trade, and its Remedy

1840: Greg, William Rathbone

William Rathbone Greg; Past and present efforts for the extinction of the African Slave Trade; 1840

William Rathbone Greg writes: "*Mr Jamieson produces ample testimony to this statement from various commanders of trading vessels to the Bights of Benin and Biafra; who concur in declaring that in 1838 and 1839, instead of a regular supply of *sixty* slave ships, which Mr Buxton's calculations would require, they have never met with more than *one*, during a detention on the coast of several months respectively. The chief stations of the Slave Trade at present seem to be the Portuguese settlements south of the line, the river Congo, Cabenda, etc, where 50 or 60 Slavers may generally be found, capable of carrying 300 to 500 Slaves each. – *Jamieson's Appeal.* 8-13. *Col Gazette,* No 82."

Past and present efforts for the extinction of the African Slave Trade

1840: MacQueen, James

James MacQueen; A Geographical Survey of Africa: Its Rivers, Lakes, Mountains, Productions, States, Populations, etc, with a Map of an Entirely New Construction, to which is Prefixed to Lord John Russell Regarding the Slave Trade and the Improvement of Africa; Fellowes; 1840

James MacQueen writes: "From Boussa, the course of the river downwards is, by compass, from north-northwest to south-southeast; but regarding the stream at this important point, our accounts are not so clear and satisfactory as could be wished, or as they might have been. Lander has given as the great breadth of the stream, at a short distance above Boussa, to be about six miles. A short space below Boussa, at the village of Songha, Clapperton gives the breadth of the river to be three-fourths the breadth of the Thames at Somerset House, when it is high water, and with a current of two miles and a half per hour; and at the ferry at the village of Comie, the breadth is said to be a quarter of a mile, the current two miles per hour, and the depth in the middle ten or twelve feet, in the dry season. This appears a diminutive and inconsistent account of the magnitude of a stream which, both above and below this place, is said to be, and known from the best authorities, to be so much greater. Lander and Clapperton had recourse, in order to account for this difference, to the opinion that the river at Boussa has large subterraneous passages, such as are to be found in calcareous countries.* This, to a certain extent, may be the case; but, after all, they may have under-estimated the breadth, and still more under-estimated the speed of the current. On this latter point, every thing depends. Clapperton mentions, that in going from Boussa to Comie, and when at some distance to the westward of the stream, he heard 'the Quorra roaring' over its rocky bed; and in another place, that he saw the stream dashing with great violence against the rocks which rose on its bank. These facts show that the current must have been very rapid. Now the quantity of water discharged by any stream through any given space, is as the square of the velocity of its current. Hence, any river with a current of four miles per hour, will discharge sixteen times as much water in the same space of time, that another river will do with a current at the rate of only one mile an hour, and one hundred times as much if the current is increased to the rate of ten miles per hour; and so on in proportion, either increasing the quantity of water discharged, or narrowing the channel. Hence we find, that the great river Congo, which is three miles broad above the cataracts, is compressed, at one of the greatest of those rapids called Sangalla, within a breadth of fifty yards.

"*The bed of the Niger near Boussa, is, according to Lander, six miles broad, and composed of banks of large round stones, bare in the dry season. Amidst the vortices of these, a vast body of water would quickly disappear. Such is the case with the great river Cuanene, in Southern Africa, the mouth of which, during the dry season, appears without water from the cause alluded to."

A Geographical Survey of Africa: Its Rivers, Lakes, Mountains, Productions, States, Populations, &c. with a Map of an Entirely New Construction, to which is …

1842: Bandinel, James

James Bandinel; Some Account of the Trade in Slaves from Africa: As Connected with Europe and America from the Introduction of the Trade Into Modern Europe Down to the Present Time: Especially with Reference to the Efforts Made by the British Government for Its Extinction; Longman, Brown, and Co; 1842

James Bandinel writes: "In the same year Diego Cam discovered the river Congo, and penetrated down to 22 degrees south latitude."

Some Account of the Trade in Slaves from Africa: As Connected with Europe and America from the Introduction of the Trade Into Modern Europe Down to the …

1843: Eldridge, Elleanor

Elleanor Eldridge; Memoirs of Elleanor Eldridge; 2nd edition; BT Albro; 1843

Elleanor Eldridge writes: "Vain were any attempt to depict the horrors of this scene. The African stood on the deck, with streaming eyes, stretching his arms out towards his own beautiful Congo; which lay, even then, distinctly visible with the ruby light of sunset, stealing, like a presence of joy, thro' bower and vale, tinging the snowy cups of a thousand lilies. There too was his own beloved Zaire, stealing away from the distant forests of mangrove and bondo, and flowing on within its lovely borders of tamarind and cedar, until, at last, it rushed into the arms of the Atlantic, troubling the placid bosom of the ocean with its tumultuous water.*

"*The river Congo, called by the native, Zaire, or Zahire, is three leagues wide at its mouth; and empties itself into the sea with so much impetuosity, that no depth can there be taken."

Memoirs of Elleanor Eldridge

1845: Tracy, Joseph

Joseph Tracy; Colonization and Missions: A History Examination of the State of Society in Western Africa, as Formed by Paganism and Muhammedanism, Slavery, the Slave Trade and Piracy, and of the Remedial Influence of Colonization and Missions; 4th edition; press of TR Marvin; 1845

Joseph Tracy writes: "In 1515, or as some say, in 1505, the Cumbas from the interior, began to make plundering incursions upon the Capez, about Sierra Leone. The Cumbas were doubtless a branch of the Giagas, another division of whom emigrated, twenty or thirty years later, to the upper region on the Congo river, and there founded the kingdom of Ansiko, otherwise called Makoko, whose king ruled over thirteen kingdoms. 'Their food,' says Rees' Cyclopedia, Art Ansiko, 'is said to be human flesh, and human bodies are hung up for sale in their shambles. Conceiving that they have an absolute right to dispose of their slaves at pleasure, their prisoners of war are fattened, killed and eaten, or sold to butchers.' Specimens of this cannibal race, from near the same region, have shown themselves within a very few years. The Cumbas, on invading the Capez, were pleased with the country, and resolved to settle there. They took possession of the most fertile spots, and cleared them of their inhabitants, by killing and eating some, and selling others to the Portuguese, who stood ready to buy them. In 1678, that is, 163 years or more from its commencement, this war was still going on.*

"*These Giagas form one of the most horribly interesting subjects for investigation, in all history. In Western Africa, they extended their ravages as far south as Benguela. Their career in that direction seems to have been arrested by the great desert, sparsely peopled by the Damaras and Namaquas, extending from Benguela to the Orange River, and presenting nothing to plunder. In 1586, the missionary Santos found them at war with the Portuguese settlements on the Zambeze. He describes their ravages, but without giving dales, along the eastern coast for a thousand miles northward to Melinda, where they were repulsed by the Portuguese. Antonio Fernandez, writing from Abyssinia in 1609, mentions an irruption of the Galae, who are said to he the same people, though some dispute their identity. These Galae, 'a savage nation, begotten of devils, as the vulgar report,' he informs us, issued from their forests and commenced their ravages a hundred years before the date of his letter; that is, about the lime of the invasion of Sierra Leone by the Cumbas. We find no express mention of their cannibalism; but in other respects they seem closely to resemble the Giagas. Thus we find them, from the commencement of the sixteenth century far into the seventeenth, ravaging the continent from the Atlantic to the Indian Ocean, and through thirty degrees of latitude. As to their original location, accounts differ. Some place it back of the northern part of Liberia. This was evidently one region from which they emigrated. Their migrations hence to Sierra Leone on the north and Congo and Benguela on the south, are recorded facts. Here, under the name of Maui, Manez, or Monou, though comparatively few in numbers, they exercised a supremacy over and received tribute from the Quojas, the Folgias, and all the maritime tribes from Sierra Leone almost to Cape Palmas. East of Cape Palmas, their cannibalism and general ferocity marked the character of the people quite down to the coast, especially along what was called the Malegentes (Bad People) and Qauqua coasts. The testimony is conclusive, that the Cumbas who invaded Sierra Leone and the Giagas of

Ansiko and Benguela were from this region. According to other accounts, their origin wits in the region on the eastern slope of the continent, from the upper waters of the Nile and the borders of Ahyssinia, extending southward across the equator. In most regions, they appeared merely as roving banditti, remaining in a country only long enough to reduce it to desolation. Every where the Giagas themselves were few, but had numerous followers, who were of the same ferocious character. Every where, except perhaps among the Galae, they had the same practice of making scars on their faces by way of ornament. Every where they practiced the same cannibalism. On taking the city of Quiloa, a little south of Zanzibar, they butchered 'three thousand Moors, for future dainties, to eat at leisure.' Every where their religion was substantially the same, consisting mainly in worshipping the devil when about to commence an expedition. They had various names, some of which have been already mentioned. In the east, they were also called Mumbos, Zimbas, and Muzimbas. In the same region, and the vicinity of Congo, they were also called Jagges, Gagas, Giachi, and it was said, called themselves Agags. Compare also, of terms still in use, the Gallas, a savage people on the south of Abyssinia, who are doubtless the Galae of Fernandez; the Golahs, formerly written Galas, north east of Monrovia, in the Monou region, of whose connection with the Giagas, however, there appears to be no other evidence; and the Mumbo Jumbo, or fictitious devil, with whom the priests overawe the superstitious in the whole region south of the Gambia. Their followers, in eastern Africa, were called Caffres; but perhaps the word was used in its original Arabic sense, as meaning infidels. Near the Congo, their followers were called Ansikos, and their principal chief, 'the great Makoko,' which some have mistaken for a national designation. Here, also, Imbe was a title of office among them, while in the east it was applied to the whole people. In Angola they were called Gindae. Whether any traces of them still remain in Eastern Africa, or around Congo and Benguela, we are too ignorant of those regions to decide. In the region of Liberia, there can be no doubt on the subject. American missionaries at Cape Palmas have seen and conversed with men from the interior, who avow without hesitation their fondness for human flesh, and their habit of eating it. On the Cavally river, the eastern boundary of Cape Palmas, the cannibal region begins some twenty, thirty or forty miles from the coast, and extends northward, in the rear of

Liberia, indefinitely. Farther east, it approaches and perhaps reaches the coast. In this region, prisoners of war and sometimes slaves are still slain for food. Here, too, slaves are sacrificed at the ratification of a treaty, and trees are planted to mark the spot and serve as records of the fact. Such trees have been pointed out to our missionaries, by men who were present when they were planted. Compare, too, the human sacrifices of Ashantee and Dahomey, and the devil-worship of all Western Africa. - But after all, were the Giagas one race of men, as cotemporary historians supposed? Or were they men of a certain character, then predominant through nearly all Africa south of the Great Desert?"

Colonization and missions: a historical examination of the state of society in western Africa, as formed by paganism and Muhammedanism, slavery, the slave ...

1847: Neilson, Peter

Peter Neilson; The Life and Adventures of Zamba: An African Negro King; and His Experience of Slavery in South Carolina; Smith, Elder and Co; 1847

Peter Neilson writes: "To the best of my calculation, I was ushered into this world of sin and woe in the year 1780. I was born in a small village situated on the south bank of the river Congo, about two hundred miles from the sea, and had the honour to claim as my father, the chief or king who ruled over this village. His empire comprised a considerable part of the surrounding country, and in his own estimation, and that of some of the neighbouring potentates, he was a personage of no small importance and dignity."

Peter Neilson continues: "My father proved as good as his word in entrusting me with a gun, and about half a year after the baboon exploit he procured me a short rifle, with which I practised for an hour or two every day, and in a month or two handled it pretty well. In my own imagination I considered myself now a match for a score of baboons or hyenas, or even for a lion of moderate size; and it was not long before my skill was put to the test. My father had appointed a regular hunting-match to take place, as several depredations had been committed upon his flocks not far from the village. About two hundred men were mustered on the occasion, and at my own urgent request I was allowed to accompany them. My father was really a very daring fellow, and as chief always considered it his duty to be foremost in danger. He, however, took good care to be well armed at all points. He had a fine double-barrelled rifle, a short cutlass by his side, a pair of pistols stuck in his belt, and an attendant close by him, carrying, for his master's use, a very strong spear, the head of which, about fifteen inches in length, was made of the finest steel, pointed, and double-edged. The shaft was about six feet long, made of lance-wood, and nearly as thick as a man's arm, so that in close encounter with any very large animal there would be no risk of its breaking. Having all assembled before daybreak at the palace, a dram of rum was served out to every man, and, each being supplied with provisions for two days, forth they went. When we had proceeded about two miles the sun arose, and by the time we had gained a certain point where the river Congo took a slight bend, one of the finest views, I believe, in Africa opened on our sight. Great part of the country before us was open, interspersed with splendid natural clumps of the teak tree, while here and there orange and palm trees adorned the scene; fields of Guinea corn, eighteen or twenty feet in height, waved in the morning breeze, the beautiful broad-leaved Indian corn, or maize, spread its waving blades in the air, and then a field of cotton might be seen. Not far distant lay our village, and near it were herds of cattle and goats, and even the labourers at work in the fields might be discerned. I forgot the hunt for a few minutes in admiring this lovely scene; and even now, when I recur to that morning, after the lapse of nearly half a century, I cannot help inwardly ejaculating, 'When, oh! when, will poor benighted, yet beautiful Africa, be brought completely and wholly under the mild and glorious influence of Christian civilization?'"

The Life and Adventures of Zamba: An African Negro King; and His Experience of Slavery in South Carolina

1848: Allen, W

W Allen, TRH Thomson; A Narrative of the Expedition to the River Niger, in 1841; Vol 1; 1848

W Allen and TRH Thomson writes: "With this great sacrifice, a step was gained to the knowledge of the course of the Niger. Although the details of the voyage were unknown, the continuity of the river was ascertained as far as Bussah, also the unexpected change of its direction from an easterly course, which puzzled all geographers, to one nearly south. This led to the wild supposition, that the waters of the Niger might discharge themselves in the River Congo or Zaire, and an expedition was sent thither under Captain Tuckey, RN. At the same time, another expedition was to follow the route of Mungo Park, in the hope of meeting at some point on the river. The usual fate of African travellers attended them; they had to encounter hardship and fever, and both failed."

A Narrative of the Expedition to the River Niger, in 1841

1848: James (Rajah of Sarawak)

James (Rajah of Sarawak), Sir James Brooke, Sir George Rodney Mundy; Narrative of events in Borneo and Celebes, down to the occupation of Labuan: from the journals of James Brooke Esq, Rajah of Sarawak, and Governor of Labaun. Together with a narrative of the operations of HMS Iris; Vol 2; J Murray; 1848 ;

James (Rajah of Sarawak), Sir James Brooke and Sir George Rodney Mundy write: "IT was early in the month of June in the year 1843, whilst I was in command of the southern division of the west African station, and cruizing in HMS Iris, off the river Congo, that a vessel was reported standing in for the land. A slaver, a slaver! at last, was the cry between the decks of the frigate, as the hands were turned up, sail quickly made, and a course shaped in the direction of the stranger. Our hopes were doomed to speedy disappointment; volumes of smoke pronounced her to be a steamer, and we soon learned by telegraphic communication, that she was in the service of her Majesty, not laden certainly with the fruits of the odious slave trade, but freighted with five months' mails direct from

England; and great riches indeed were these to men who had passed eight dreary months cruizing on this desolate shore, without news of home or of happy England, and without a single prize to vary the monotony of the scene."

Narrative of events in Borneo and Celebes, down to the occupation of Labuan: from the journals of James Brooke esq., rajah of Sarāwak, and governor of …

1848: Matson, Henry James

Henry James Matson; Remarks on the slave trade and African squadron; Vol 10; 2nd edition; 1848

Henry James Matson writes: "In my report to the Admiralty, in 1843, on the coast of Africa, which was printed in the first report of the Slave Trade Committee, I thus describe that part of the coast: - 'Between Cape Lopez (latitude 0 degrees 36 minutes) and Mayumba (latitude 3 degrees 22 minutes) there is no Slave trade, nor any trade whatever; the country is impassable, it is very thinly populated, and the natives are less civilized than on any other part of the coast. This effectually prevents any communication between the Bights and the south-west coast of Africa. Between Mayumba and the River Congo, the slave trade has been very briskly and successfully carried on for many years, principally by Spaniards from Havana.' Such was the state of things in 1843, and I am informed by officers, lately returned from the coast, that it is the same to this day. In saying that there was no slave trade between Cape Lopez and Mayumba, I did not say that it was impossible to build a barracoon on the beach; I am informed that barracoons are now built there, for the temporary reception of slaves, which are transported along shore in launches, from the slave factories at Cabenda and Loango, and shipped from thence, out of the way of Her Majesty's cruisers. This proceeding was indeed attempted when I was on that coast. Captain Birch's evidence goes entirely to prove the correctness of my description of the coast in 1843, *viz,* that there is plenty of Slave trade between Congo and Mayumba, but that it cannot be established between Mayumba and Cape Lopez; for almost in the same breath that he volunteers a contradiction to some supposed statement of mine, he says, (2244-2247) that, 'there are numerous factories at Cabenda, but no barracoons.' Where, then, are the barracoons? Captain Birch himself answers the question: 'they have gone down farther to the northward, nearer Cape Lopez. There are no slaves shipped at Cabenda, they are shipped by the men who actually live in Cabenda, but they transport their slaves coastwise,' That is, they run along shore to the northward, for which the wind is always fair, and ship their slaves out of sight of one of her Majesty's cruisers. But this proceeding can, I think, be always frustrated by the exercise of ordinary vigilance, supposing the cruiser not to be nailed to the same spot."

Henry James Matson continues: "I once passed two days in the house of a slave merchant, thirty-five miles up the river Congo, and visited his establishment thirty miles still higher up: I received from him a good deal of information respecting the country, and the social condition of its people. He was a most singular man: there was a mixture of benevolence and ferocity in his disposition which one could scarcely comprehend, - benevolent by nature, which his education and mode of life could not entirely change. His name was Alphonse Meynier; a Frenchman by birth, and educated for the medical profession; he commenced life as the surgeon of a slave vessel, and on the deaths of nearly all the medical officers in Captain Owen's surveying expedition in 1827, he received from that officer an acting appointment as Assistant-surgeon in her Majesty's navy; but this he soon relinquished for the more lucrative employment as agent to a Slave trading house at Havana, and which he had then held for the previous ten or twelve years; he left Africa in 1842, when the slave factories were destroyed, returned in two or three years afterwards, and is, I believe, there still. He was not only a shrewd, but a very intelligent man; he was a practical philosopher; he did not express any wish to see the Slave trade abolished, as he thought, with his brother Cliffe, that it was the most profitable trade under the sun. He considered it, however, to be the curse of Africa, which the British nation would one day succeed in eradicating; he spoke in admiration of the people, who he said were the mildest and most inoffensive that he had ever known; in mildness of disposition they would bear a comparison with any European nation; crime, or what they considered crime, was scarcely known among them. These qualities of the Congos are well known on the other side of the

Atlantic; they are delicate, and therefore not suited to field labour, or any hard work; but they are chosen for domestic servants both in Cuba and Brazil."

Henry James Matson continues: "Taking alone into consideration the suppression of the slave trade, the stations should be divided either by the 3rd, 7th, or 16th degree of south latitude. Between Cape Lopez (latitude 0 degrees 36 minutes) and Mayumba (latitude 3 degrees 22 minutes), there is no slave trade, nor any trade whatever; the country is impassable, it is very thinly populated, and the natives are less civilized than on any other part of the coast. This effectually prevents any communication between the Bights and the south-west coast of Africa. Between Mayumba and the river Congo the slave trade has been very briskly and successfully carried on for many years, principally by Spaniards from Havannah. This part of the coast might certainly belong to either station, but it were better that all cruisers to the southward of 3 degrees south should be under the immediate command of the same officer, who, by having a number of vessels at his disposal, could ensure the coast being equally guarded; and in case of a cruiser being in want of provisions, she might be supplied or relieved by one whose services could be better spared, instead of leaving an important post unguarded. It is moreover absolutely impossible for the senior officer in the Bights personally to attend to this part of the station; he must entrust it to one of his subordinates - in fact make it a distinct station. Should it, however, be necessary for other reasons to attach this part of the coast (from Mayumba to Congo) to the northern station, another good division might be made by the river Congo, or the seventh degree of south latitude.

"The coast between the river Congo and Ambriz is another waste and sterile tract, almost destitute of fresh water, and where there is no trade whatever. At Ambriz (latitude 7 degrees 52 minutes) begins the Portuguese slave trade, and near this spot will always be the principal market for slaves, roads converging to that place from all parts of the interior, and even from the opposite shore of Mozambique."

Remarks on the slave trade and African squadron

1849: Beke, Charles Tilstone

Charles Tilstone Beke; On the Geographical Distribution of the Languages of Abessinia and the neighbouring countries. [With a map. Reprinted from the Edinburgh New Philosophical Journal.]; Neill & Co; 1849

Charles Tilstone Beke writes: "Mr Robertson, in his *Notes on Africa* (London, 1819), pp 353-354, when treating of the natives of the south bank of the river Congo, says: 'The opinion that these, or any other people on this [the west] coast, are Anthropophagi, is ridiculous. One of the traders at Bonny did, indeed, once tell me so plausible a story concerning the Quas eating those who fell into their power, that I was half inclined to believe him. But subsequent inquiry convinced me that there was no truth whatever in it. ... The Portuguese having taken so much trouble to impress other nations with the dreadful effects of man-eating, *they, of course, consider this country of some value;* but from their not having been devoured themselves, it seems other animal food is plentiful; or, perhaps, the aboriginal inhabitants think the Portuguese rather coarse meat, and like cattle or fish better.'"

On the Geographical Distribution of the Languages of Abessinia and the neighbouring countries.[With a map. Reprinted from the Edinburgh New ...

1849: Wilkes, Charles

Charles Wilkes; Voyage Round the World: Embracing the Principal Events of the Narrative of the United States Exploring Expedition in One Volume: Illustrated with One Hundred and Seventy-eight Engravings on Wood; Geo W Gorton; 1849

Charles Wilkes writes: "The inhabitants of the town of Embomma, on the north bank of the river Congo, are distinguished by the teeth being filed so that each tooth forms a point."

Charles Wilkes continues: "Of the exact geographical position of the Mundjola, no definite information was known. The part of the continent which they are said to inhabit is still unexplored; the account which one of them gave Mr Hale was, that he had been three days with his captors in canoes, from his native place, M'te, situated on the great river Muote, before reaching Loango, where he embarked. It is probable that M'te is in the interior, two or three hundred miles northeast of Loango, and that he was brought to the coast by the Zaire river; but in this wild, unexplored ground, all is yet conjecture. The next town or tribe to M'te he called Mudimbe."

Voyage Round the World: Embracing the Principal Events of the Narrative of the United States Exploring Expedition in One Volume: Illustrated with One …

1850: Appleyard, John Whittle

John Whittle Appleyard; The Kafir Language: Comprising a Sketch of Its History; which Includes a General Classification of South African Dialects, Ethnographical and Geographical: Remarks Upon Its Nature: and a Grammar; Wesleyan Missionary Society; 1850

John Whittle Appleyard writes: "*The Portuguese were probably the first Europeans who visited Congo. An expedition under Diego Cam discovered the river Zaire about the year 1488. On ascending it, 'the shores proved to be filled with people exceedingly black, and speaking a language which, though Diego knew those spoken on other parts of the coast, was wholly unintelligible to him.' – Historical account of Discoveries and Travels in Africa, by Hugh Murray, FRSE. Vol 1: p 64."

The Kafir Language: Comprising a sketch of its history; which includes a general classification of South African dialects, ethnographical and geographical: …

1851: Smith, John

John Smith (Surgeon and Trading Captain); Trade and Travel in the Gulph of Guinea, Western Africa, with an account of the manners, habits, customs, and religion of the inhabitants; Simpkin & Marshall; 1851

John Smith writes: "The chief exportations from the south-west coast of Africa, in the neighbourhood of the river Congo, are slaves, ivory, gum copal, and bees' wax. The contraband trade is carried on by Spaniards, Portuguese, and Brazilians, the legitimate trade, chiefly by Englishmen."

Trade and Travels in the Gulph of Guinea, Western Africa, with an account of the manners, habits, customs, and religion of the inhabitants

1854: Cooley, William Desborough

William Desborough Cooley; Claudius Ptolemy and the Nile: or, An inquiry into that geographer's real merits and speculative errors, his knowledge of Eastern Africa and the authenticity of the Mountains of the Moon; Parker; 1854

William Desborough Cooley writes: "The river where it leaves the lake has a breadth exceeding 200 yards, but it soon undergoes a remarkable change*. And here it will be necessary to insist on the remark, that, in the case of rivers, velocity is an equivalent of magnitude. A river becomes full and large by accumulation, and, of course, other circumstances remaining constant, it is larger the less rapidly it runs off. Consequently, a small torrent may become a great river; and again, a great river may shrink to a small torrent. A remarkable example of such change occurs in the river Zaire. This, near its mouth, is a great river, five or six miles wide, very deep, and with a strong current. At the falls, 120 miles up, it appears but an insignificant stream; but again, above the falls, it becomes a noble river, one or two miles wide, and uniformly deep. So great indeed seemed the disparity between the torrent hurrying down the rocks, and the broad majestic stream above and below the falls, that Capt Tuckey was driven to conjecture, that the real passage of the river was underground - an absurd and wholly needless supposition. In like manner, an attempt has been made to represent the Abai as a contemptible rivulet, quite unworthy of figuring as the parent of the great river of the plains: and, to compensate for the river thus lost to view through imperfect insight into nature, another has been substituted for it, derived wholly from the misconstruction of authorities.

"*M Ant D'Abbaddie (Bulletin, 1845, p 346) estimated its width, at the end of June, to be 200 metres (656 feet), but Bruce found it in May, above half a mile wide, 'deep and broad, and rolling a prodigious quantity of water'. (Trav, vol V, pp 80, 111)."

Claudius Ptolemy and the Nile: or, An inquiry into that geographer's real merits and speculative errors, his knowledge of Eastern Africa and the authenticity of ...

1854: Maitland, James A

James A Maitland; The Cabin Boy's Story: A Semi-nautical Romance, Founded on Fact; Cottage library; Garrett; 1854

James A Maitland writes: "*Aguardiente* was the first thing asked for, and then tobacco in the leaf, both of which were moderately supplied. On being questioned by the captain, the chiefs informed him that the whole line of coast from Majumba as far south as Loanda had been for many weeks narrowly watched by two British men-of-war, and King Kettle had found it necessary to remove his slaves to Quaddah, a village on the Zaire river, beyond where it was unnavigable by any thing but native canoes, and a distance of seven days' journey from the coast, in consequence of the men-of-war's boats having pulled a great many miles up the river."

The cabin boy's story: a semi-nautical romance, founded on fact

1855: Purdy, John

John Purdy; Alexander George Findlay, editor; The new sailing directory for the Ethiopic or southern Atlantic ocean; 4th edition; 1855

John Purdy writes: "**The RIVER CONGO, ZAIRE, or COUANGO,** as it is usually named, is called by the inhabitants of the country *Moienza-Enzaddi*. It is said to have a course of 600 leagues, and it is supposed to rise from the Lake Akelounda. But this is quite conjectural, for its course is unknown beyond 100 leagues from its mouth.* The coast was explored by Captain Tuckey, by order of the English Government, and was surveyed, in 1825, by Captain A Vidal, RN.

"[*The mystery of its origin, however, appears to be on the eve of being cleared up, as Dr Livingston, in his remarkable journey in 1853-4, from the neighbourhood of L N'gami to St Paul de Loanda, through Cassange, crossed some streams which, flowing to the northwest, were supposed to be the upper portions of the Congo.]

"Its principal known tributaries are the Wambre, which joins it in about latitude 6 degrees south, longitude 14 degrees east; and the River Lumini, which enters it about 43 leagues about the Falls of Yellala, which are about 112 miles from the mouth of the Congo. These two rivers appear to have a southerly direction. The course of the Congo above them appears to be north-northeast; below them, and after their junction with it, it has several bends, but chiefly flows in a south 60 degrees west direction for a distance of 68 miles. It is joined here by a considerable number of secondary streams.

"The Congo brings down an immense volume of water, which has hollowed for itself a narrow bed, a very variable depth. In many places there is no bottom at 200 fathoms. Forty miles from its mouth its waters are only partially mingled with those of the sea, and sometimes 9 miles out they are still quite fresh.

"The main body of the stream of this mighty river is indicated by floating masses of bamboo, and debris of all kinds, which it carries far out to sea. The velocity of the current is said to range at from 4 to 8 miles an hour. It is high water, at full and change, at 4 hours 30 minutes at the mouth of the Congo.

"The stream of the River Congo is felt a great distance out at sea, and ships which cross it, in going to the North or to the South, ought therefore to guard against it. It is stated that 300 miles out the water is discoloured, and that the current of the river is perceptible at that distance, which is not impossible.

"The Congo is only 7 ½ miles wide between the West point of its entrance, called *Shark Point,* and the East point, called *Boolambemba.* The former bears west by north from the latter.

"It is 24 miles from Red Point, described before, to Shark Point, and 29 miles between Red Point and Cape Padrao, the southwest point of the mouth of the river.

"Within these four points the mouth of the Congo is funnel shaped, being very wide in its West part, but considerably contracted between Shark Point and Point Boolambemba, and the bank of Mona Mazea still further narrows it.

"The banks of the river, formed of alluvial deposits, are covered with mangroves, one species of which grows to a considerable size; it has a straight stem, sometimes 100 feet high, supported by an arch of roots, which rise as much as 20 feet from the ground. The spaces between these giant mangroves are filled with various kinds of trees of smaller growth, among which are a good many palm trees. Other parts of the banks are lined with common mangroves of low growth. The country near the river is low and marshy; but at some distance inland may be seen some wooded hills. Shark Point, which is covered with the tall mangroves of which we have been speaking, is considerably higher than the land on the right and left of it.

"The rising of the Congo occurs six weeks after the commencement of the rainy season, that is, about the middle of November. It then rises 8 feet 9 inches above its ordinary level. The stream becomes very rapid, and bears along with it floating islands, formed of the roots of plants of all kinds, covered with bamboos and grass; these are very dangerous for ships under sail, and especially for those at anchor. Some of them are more than 100 yards long.

"The rains, no doubt, have much to do with the rising of the river; still we do not think they are the sole cause of it, but that it may be partially attributed to the strong sea breezes which blow at this period, and necessarily contribute to retard the flow of the waters, and to dam them up, as it were, in the upper parts of the river. Indeed, in the years 1845-6-7, the rains were very trifling on the Congo coast, yet the Congo did not rise the less, though it was not so strong as usual.

"It is a subject of regret that navigators, who have had occasion to enter the Congo, and to remain there some time, have not furnished us with some information about the tides. For all our researches, we can only give a few observations, which are far from being sufficient. We will speak first of the currents outside the mouth of the river.

"The waters which come from a river, in running out to sea, usually diverge somewhat from the original course, and join the general current which sets along the coast, at a certain distance out. The point of junction of the two streams varies, as to its distance from the entrance of the river, according as the waters of the latter have more or less speed, or the current itself is more or less strong.

"Although the rise or fall of the level of the waters is often perceptible at the junction of the streams, the effect of the tides is not more marked than usual.

"At the mouth of the River Congo, the commander of the French frigate *Venus,* in a voyage to Kabenda in 1784, mentions having felt a strong current about 21 miles out, to the North of Cape Padrao. Being an anchor in 20 fathoms, the current was estimated by the log to set at the rate of 3 miles an hour towards the north-northwest. In the centre of the stream of the Congo the captain of the *Venus* estimated the rate of it at 6 miles an hour; and at the time he was off the entrance of the river, the stream constantly set out of it, notwithstanding the effects of the tide. This observation is important; and we shall see hereafter how it may be turned to account.

"Off the mouth of the Congo, beyond the distance of 35 miles, the currents set to the north-northwest, North of the parallel of Boolambemba; to the west-northwest, on the parallel of the Point; and to the southwest, South of the parallel of Cape Padrao. Their speed is very variable, and attains often, even at this distance, a rate of 3 or 4 miles an hour. Sometimes, at spring tides and the dry season, the strength of the current may be crossed without feeling its influence.

"The waters of the Congo are very much discoloured with a yellowish red tinge; they are covered with foam and rubbish of every description. Very frequently, South of Cape Padrao, along the shore, the sea is very much agitated, and shows in overfalls. At 40 miles out from the mouth of the river the waters become of a dark and blackish tint. They are brackish at this distance.

"You must not enter the River Congo without a commanding sea breeze, which usually rises about 9 hours or 10 hours in the morning, and blows from the south-southwest to the west-southwest. The stream in the river has been found, as we have said, to run at the rate of more than 5 miles an hour. The direction of the stream is from Point Boolambemba on to the Mona Mazea bank, and runs along the coast up towards Red Point. Its course on this side is then North, or northwest, or north-northwest, when near the right bank of the river. In the middle of the river, between Point Boolambemba and the left bank, the stream sets to the West; and near the left bank it appears to follow the course of the bank, *ie,* West or southwest. In Diegos Bay, which is an indication of the left bank, South of Point Shark, it sets towards the North as far up as this point, which it rounds, and on the meridian of which it takes a west-southwest direction. Within the river, above Point Boolambemba, the current follows the direction of the banks.

"Moreover, in the Congo, a rapid surface current, and an under one running in an opposite direction, is sometimes found to occur. In the instance in which this was observed, the ship, being becalmed, and drifting with the stream, was only carried at the rate of 1 mile or 1 ½ miles an hour, although the surface current appeared to be moving at the rate of 4 or 5 miles.*

"[**M de la Condamine* mentions an analogous case. On the 28th August, 1743, the tide was felt at Pauxis, situated 100 leagues from the mouth of the River Amazon; the stream was moving seawards all the time, but still the level of the water rose, a fact which can only be explained by the existence of an under current.

"'When at anchor myself,' continues M de Kerhallet, '10 miles off the River Pongo, I observed a similar phenomenon. The surface current always set to the northwest, according to the log, although the depth of water varied regularly and gradually, according to the ebb and flow of the tide.']

"There is no masceret (bore) or *pororoca* at the entrance of the Congo, since this river appears to have at its mouth a bar, on which there is probably a depth of 20 fathoms, according to Captain Owen. Thirteen miles from Cape Padrao, the greatest depth that this officer found was 44 fathoms.

"At the time of the new and full moon there are dangerous tide races, which cause the sea to break violently on a portion of the Mona Mazea bank.

"*Between Red Point and Point Boolambemba* there are to be found, in the midst of the palm woods, the villages of *Ma-Camma* and *Mona Mazea,* the former 17 ½ miles, the latter 3 ½ miles, from Point Boolambemba; then 11 ½ miles from the same point, the *River Dos-Mosquitos,* which may be recognized by a remarkable wood on its right bank, called the *Fetishe Wood*. Lastly, 1 ½ miles to the North of the same point is *Pirate's Creek,* with a tolerably wide entrance; the village of Mona Mazea stands on the point of the left bank of this strand. In the mouths of these two creeks, which often afford shelter to slavers, are found 12 feet of water. Dos-Mosquitos River is very narrow, and divides into two streams a short distance from its mouth.

"POINT BOOLAMBEMBA, also called *Fathomless Point,* is a low point, with a clump of trees a little higher than those around on its southern part. Beyond the point is seen the plain of the River Congo, running east by south, low, woody, and intersected by numberless creeks or rivulets.

"A little inland a range of hills runs parallel with the shore from Red Point to Point Boolambemba, in a line with which it terminates. These hills, which are moderately high, appear from the offing to form the shore, which at their foot is lined with thick trees. Some single, scattered trees are seen on the top of these hills. With Boolambemba Point bearing east ½ north, and Shark Point south-southeast, at a distance of 18 miles from the former, and low coast is just distinguishable by the line of trees upon it, which have open intervals here and there. But to the right is very distinctly seen the rounded and pretty steep declivity which terminates the hills in the interior.

"More to the South is seen the low, woody country on the left bank of the river, the trees appearing in the water at this distance; then, on the right, Shark Point is easily recognized by its tall mangroves.

"SHARK POINT, as we have stated, is the extremity of a kind of peninsula, low and covered with trees, which stretches out to the northeast. Some lofty mangroves form a clump, remarkable for their height, at the extremity of this point.

"To the East of Shark Point the coast trends inwards, and forms a bay, which is filled by banks with only 9 feet water on them. There is a narrow channel through them, caused by the flowing of several watercourses into the bottom of the bay, which is called *Sonhio,* or *Diegos Bay.*

"Shark Point is steep to, and near the sandy beach which skirts it you find 7 fathoms, then 26 fathoms. But a little to the East of its meridian you find, quite close to the sandy beach, 2 fathoms; and in its eastern part 4 and 5 fathoms close in shore. You can pass it within one-third or even one-quarter of a mile.

"At 2 2/3 miles to the west by south ¼ south of Shark Point, the shore forms a gently rounded eminence, covered with tall trees, called *Turtle Corner,* and 3 miles west-southwest from this point is Cape Padrao.

"CAPE PADRAO, OR PADRON, seen from the North, 7 miles distant, has the appearance of a perpendicular cliff, which runs down to the beach; just above the beach are some woods. The cliff forming the cape rises rapidly, with a rounded elevation; its summit is covered with a stunted vegetation, apparently of grass and brushwood. The colour of the cliff is remarkable for its rosy tint rather than red. Cape Padron is called by the Portuguese *Mouta Secca,* or Dry Thicket Point.

"The land of Cape Padrao is low, and the sea washes the foot of the cliff. All the shore is safe hereabouts, and you can cruise along in it 10 or 13 fathoms.

"When you come in sight of Cape Padrao from the South, you may see to the northeast the land on the right bank of the river. From a distance you may often fancy you see a town and houses built in a semicircle, an illusion caused by a confused mass of rocks, which have this deceptive appearance. From Cape Padrao the land slopes down to Shark Point.

"Between Point Boolambemba and Shark Point the entrance of the River Congo is well defined, and is, as we have said, 7 ½ miles wide. The right bank of the river then takes an east by south direction, forming at Point Boolambemba a very acute angle, while the left bank trends inwards gently, describing a semicircle.

"In nearing either bank the depths vary from 6 to 8 fathoms, except near Point Boolambemba, where there is no bottom at 93 fathoms, one third of a mile out.

"In mid-channel there is no bottom with 80 to 100 fathoms at the mouth of the river, and for a distance of about 25 miles up the stream. This circumstance renders the navigation very difficult, and sometimes even dangerous. It will, therefore, be always prudent to get a local pilot, from Kabenda or elsewhere, to take the ship into the Congo.

"When you want to go any distance up the river, it will be necessary, whichever direction you come from, to keep close along the left or South bank; so that, coming from the North, you will have to cross the strength of the steam. We will explain how this is to be effected, so as not to be driven out to sea by the current.

"Coming from the North, it will be sufficient, to enable you to cross the stream, to have a fresh and settled breeze from the southwest or west-southwest. When we speak of out at sea, we suppose that you are 150 or 200 miles from the coast, at which distance it is said that the current from the Congo attains at certain periods a rate of 2 or 3 miles an hour. It is not known at what distance this current, which usually has a northwest or north-northwest direction, becomes united with the Atlantic current, which sets along the coast from the Cape of Good Hope; but as the latter has a speed of not more than 24 or 26 miles in 24 hours, it is possible that the current of the Congo may be felt at a very great distance.

"The second course for crossing the river in coming from the North, and the one generally taken, is to tack along the shore between Kabenda and Red Point, without leaving the bank of soundings. When you have made Red Point, then anchor, if you find you cannot make way. But if the sea breeze is favourable, you must calculate so as to get clear across the stream while this breeze lasts, and to reach the left bank of the river before it drops. So that even if you have reached Red Point, and are not sure of having time enough to cross the current, it will be much better to anchor somewhere off the point, and wait for the sea breeze next day, and then to weigh as soon as it is will set in; this breeze usually rises about 9 or 10 o'clock in the morning, and blows from the southwest or west-southwest till evening.

"If you only want to proceed down to the coast to southwards, without entering the river, after you have got across the stream, you will keep on your course as long as you have a fresh sea breeze; and in case it is nearly ceasing when you have traversed the current, the better way will be anchor to the southwest of Cape Padrao, 3 or 4 miles out, according to the distance you have got from the mouth of the river, and there wait for the next day's sea breeze to carry you on along the coast southwards.

"In this course you must steer in the following manner; on leaving the parallel of Red Point, at a distance of 9 miles from the point, set the head of the vessel on the Shark Point or Cape Padrao, as far as the parallel of Pirate's Creek. Here the streams set to the north-northwest, and it will be sufficient to coast along about 9 miles out to clear the Mona Mazea Bank in 10 or 11 fathoms, in which depth you should keep; the course will be about south by east.

"Then, when you get on a line with Pirate's Creek, or even before, according as you feel the force of the current greater or less, or a tendency in it to set towards the west-northwest and West, bring the vessel up as if you intended to enter the river, steering right for the middle of the open space between Point Boolambemba and Shark Point. You will in this way get across the strongest part of the stream, and when you bear up for the left bank, haul your wind and steer so as to be carried on the South shore, till within 3 or 4 miles, and then anchor as you please.

"If you want to enter the Congo, you must still anchor in the southwest of Cape Padrao, and await the sea breeze to carry you in; unless you are in time to double Shark Point, and to anchor on the left bank to the East of this point.

"You must never attempt to cross in the evening, for it is seldom that you would in this case have time to clear the main stream during the continuance of the sea breeze; and if it were to drop before you reach the left side, you would be inevitably carried out to sea.

"Coming from the South, when you have sighted Cape Padrao, you may bring up 3 miles off, which may be done without danger. If you arrive at night, anchor to the southwest of the cape, and wait till morning for the passage across. As soon as the sea breeze becomes settled, then weigh, and with the cape bearing east-northeast or northeast by east, you will be in the most advantageous course for clearing the stream. Keep this course till you begin to find yourself in the bed of the stream; then bring the cape to bear northeast by north, or north-northeast, and keep the lead going, to be sure of the moment you get on to the Mona Mazea sands on the right bank.

"When you are going to Kabenda, you must keep off the Mona Mazea Bank; and on leaving the Congo run out to sea for about 40 miles from its mouth, before you put the ship's head to the North, in order to avoid a bank which is not marked on the charts, and which, beginning at Red Point, extends 9 miles to the West of the point, running up to the North to join Point Palmas, the South point of the Bay of Kabenda. You must also take notice of the current which sets to the north-northeast at the rate of 1 mile an hour, sometimes more, according to the strength of the wind.

"The chief markets and most populous places are a long way up the river, near the boundary of the kingdom of Embomma, the capital of which, called Banza Embomma, is situated on the right bank of the River Congo. On the same side, near the Falls of Yellala, is Inga; and further on, Condo-Yongo. On the left bank, going from the mouth, you find the villages of Pinda, Seenda, and Banza-Sonhio, on the Alligator River, which, they say, runs up to the town of Banza-Congo, or San Salvador, a place where the Portuguese formerly carried on a great trade. Alligator River is on the left bank of the Congo, about 11 ½ miles from Shark Point. The town of San Salvador is about 40 miles inland.

"Proceeding further up the river, you come to the towns of Batta, Sundi, Condi, and Canga, near the left bank. The two latter are near the outlets of the Rivers Wambu and Lumini. The largest of these villages has barely 600 or 800 inhabitants, a number much less than stated by the French and Portuguese missionaries. The chiefs called themselves 'chenoux'; the collectors of imports are 'mafoux'. The people in the higher parts of the river are mild, hospitable, and very lazy.

"The brief directions for entering the river, as given by *Captain Vidal,* RN, are – 'It is necessary to approach the river from the southward, and anchor near Point Padron, until the sea breeze sets in strong enough to stem the current round Shark's Point, and proceed up, keeping the southern shore abroad. Latitude of Shark's Point 6 degrees 4 minutes 36 seconds south, longitude 12 degrees 12 minutes 30 minutes east. Variation, 21 degrees 42 minutes west.'

"REMARKS AND DIRECTIONS, BY THE FRENCH MISSIONARIES, IN 1773.

"'CONGO RIVER forms a most impetuous current at its mouth; in order to cross over that current, when coming from the South towards Kabenda, you go along shore, at 1 ½ or 2 leagues' distance, in 10 fathoms of water: the coast is low, and covered with woods.

"'If you should happen to be on the South side of this current, and night coming on, you must come to and anchor to the southwest of Cape Padron, 1 ½ or 2 leagues off the coast, and wait till the breeze shall be formed next day; it would be hazardous at attempt the passage during the night. The breeze commonly begins at 9 or 10 o'clock, and blows from south-southwest to west-southwest. You direct the head of the ship from east-northeast to northeast, to encounter the current in the most advantageous manner, and keep it so till you begin to be in the bed or channel or the river, when you put the head to north-northeast, having a continual recourse to the lead. The water runs with such force in the middle of the channel, that it carries away the lead; and you would attempt in vain to moor, if you were overtaken there in a calm.

"'When you are past this impetuous current, you find from 16 or 13 fathoms of water, and then must come nearer the land, approaching it within 1 ½ leagues; you are to keep in 6 and 8 fathoms, without ever coming under 5, from fear of some sandbanks, on which there are not more than 15 feet of water; besides, by keeping in the above depths, you find everywhere an even ground, where you can safely anchor in case of a calm. So soon as you can descry Kabenda Hills, you may steer northeast, provided you should keep always in the same ground.

"'Within 4 or 5 leagues of Kabenda you may perceive the ships which lie in the Road, over a very low slip of land, which is called Palm trees Point: should you not be inclined to come immediately into the Road, the ships are to be brought east-southeast, and Palm trees Point south-southwest, and then you come to an anchor in 5 or 6 fathoms, oozy sand.'

"REMARKS ON THE ZAHIR, BY MR GEORGE MAXWELL.

"'VESSELS sailing out of Congo River should take Shark Point close on board, and, anchoring under it, supply themselves with fish, which they may do abundantly in a couple of hauls with the seine. But this coming to Shark Point should never be attempted till the sea breeze sets in, lest the irregular eddy current running off it should render the vessel ungovernable, and sweep her over on the Mona Mazea or northwest shore, the bank of which should be approached no nearer than in 5 fathoms; and it is dangerous to anchor there when a heavy swell sets in about the full and change, the current running north-northwest on the edge of that bank, at the rate of 7 miles per hour.

"'Vessels intended for the Congo should be provided with a mooring chain, or chain cables; the water of that river having the quality of rotting cables in a short space of time.

"'About six weeks after the commencement of the rainy season (that is, from the middle of December to the latter end of April), you find in the river 9 feet more water than the common depth; and it has a very rapid current, which brings along with its numbers of floating islands, some of them 100 yards in length, composed of fibrous roots, and covered with grass, which renders it very dangerous to vessels at anchor when tornadoes happen, which are also very frequent.'

"REMARKS FROM THE NARRATIVE OF CAPTAIN WF OWEN.

"1825. Dec 24 – 'Entered the Congo, and for six successive days in vain attempted to stem its rapid stream; but on the 1st of January, 1826, the sea breeze being stronger than usual, we succeeded in passing Shark Point, where the current always runs with the greatest velocity, and in about thirty hours anchored at 25 miles from the southern entrance of the river. Here the Congo (Zahir) was not more than 1 ½ miles in width; and, at a short distance above, a broad sandbank divided the stream into two narrow but deep channels.

"'The banks on each side above Shark Point are low and swampy, and covered principally with two different kinds of mangrove; the one a low grovelling bush, and the other a stately tree, resting on a forest of roots, upwards of 20 feet above the ground, the trunk often rising to the height of 100 more. Most of them are perfectly, and if the wood were a little lighter, they would be admirably, adapted for masts. The spaces between these lofty trees are filled up by a variety of smaller growth, but with beautiful and luxuriant foliage, among which are many of the palm kind.

"'The great body of water discharged by the Congo has scooped out a channel for itself, narrow, but immensely deep, above Shark Point, seldom more than a mile across, varying in depth from 200 to 45 fathoms. The great force of the current in the river is apparently but superficial, as when drifting out, during a calm, the vessel was so much retarded by the current below that the superficial one was running past apparently at the rate of 1 ½ miles in the hour, when its real velocity was about 4 miles.

"'Many floating islands were seen coming down the river, formed of rushes, reeds, and long grass, and frequently covered with birds. Vessels are sometimes deceived by these, which occasionally drift a long way to seaward. The country at the mouth of the Congo is apparently very fertile, and presents many agreeable views; a range of high lands, covered with clusters of trees, extending some distance along its course.

"'The people of Kabenda give the inhabitants of the mouth of the Congo a bad character for treachery and cruelty. They stated that whenever an opportunity offered for attacking a boat, either of Europeans or Africans, they would kill those who were likely to be unprofitable, and preserve the remainder for slaves, or to be ransomed. If they made any resistance, a death of torture was inflicted on them all; but if allowed to live, they were stripped naked, made to procure their own food in what manner they could, and kept at hard labour in the most servile duties. This character of these people was subsequently confirmed; while those inhabiting the shores at a few miles from the mouth were described, as Captain Tucker had found them, a harmless, inoffensive race.'

"DIRECTIONS BY CAPTAIN TUCKER, RN.

"The passage up may be made at all times of the day, with the flood tide, or against the ebb, if the sea breeze be strong enough. The best time for a stranger to make it is certainly with the first of the sea breeze; though, on taking HMS *Wolverine* to the shoals a second time, I went up in the afternoon, and on the third time I went up in the evening, passing the lower shoals, and anchored, at 8 hours pm, close to a slave vessel lying between the two lower shoals.

"The passage up should be made on and close to the left bank, until you arrive at the lower shoal, about 20 miles from the mouth of the river, where a spit with 2, 1 ¾, 1 ½, and 1 fathom on it runs off the left bank about a cable's length, which shows itself at low water, by the smoothness of the water on the lower part of it. From thence you should steer diagonally across the river, keeping her head well up, for a low, sandy, and green island on the right bank, keeping close to the lower edge of the lower shoal in 7, 7, and 9 fathoms until you arrive near the island, when you must steer up close to the right bank, carrying your lower studding sail booms over the bushes, having 6, 7, 8, 9, and 10 fathoms, except a small shoal with 4 fathoms, when you must edge off a little, so as to pass it about a vessel's breadth from the bank. Then you must steer along the bank again until you arrive off Punta da Linha, and anchor in 4 and 4 ½ fathoms, a mile above which the river is not navigable for vessels.

"The passage down is rather dangerous; but I think, by attention and prudence, it may be always made with safety. The usual passage down the river is crossing to the left bank above the shoals, and passing between them and the bank; but should only be attempted with a commanding sea breeze, with which, even, it is necessary to keep the ship's head well up the river, and allow the stream to set you gradually down until you gain the left bank; when you must drop down close to the bank in 4, 3 ½, and 3 fathoms, either by kedging or under sail; I prefer the latter.

"The danger of crossing the river in coming down arises from the wind falling or lulling, and the vessel, in consequence (if not brought up very smartly with her anchor), being set by the stream upon the upper edge of the shoal; which has caused the total loss of many vessels, and the loss of rudder of many others. In light winds I should, therefore, recommend the vessel to be taken down by the sweeps, on the right bank, with the kedge ready to be dropped, and the boats down ready for towing, until you arrive on the lower edge of the lower shoal; when, if there be no sea breeze, it will be necessary to bring the vessel up with a bower anchor in 7, 8, or 9 fathoms, to avoid the shoal running along the right bank, over which the stream sets with great force. But if the sea breeze be commanding, you may cross over to the left bank by keeping the vessel's head well up the river until you get well over; when you may either back, or fill, or work down, standing from 4 fathoms on the left bank into not less than 7 fathoms on the right bank, until past Boolambemba Point and Spit, when you must not stand into less than 4 fathoms.

"With respect to the shoal of 3 ½, 3 ¼ fathoms, on the *Mona Mazea Bank*, in the mouth of the river, which I have laid down, I am of opinion that it is a very late formation, and will prove very dangerous to vessels crossing the river as I did. Steering well up the river from the southward to cross over to Cape Padron, carrying 7 and 8 fathoms, I suddenly got into 3 ½, 3 ¼ fathoms, along which I ran, carrying 7 and 6 fathoms on the port side, and 3 ½ and 3 ¼ fathoms on the starboard side, for about more than 3 ship's lengths.

"I am of opinion that the whole of the Mona Mazea Bank is rising fast, from the deposit of mud out of the river, and from the sand thrown over by the heavy swell which often sets it upon it.

"It is high water, at full and change, 4 hours 3 minutes; variation, one point and three-quarters.

"REMARKS BY CAPTAIN EH BUTTERFIELD, RN.

"'The depth of water in the Congo differs very much from the sounds laid in the chart of that river, and several banks exist which are not laid down at all; but we had no opportunity of surveying them. The water in the stream, in 14 fathoms, is very good; the tide running from 6 to 7 knots. In 5 fathoms, near the shore, where we anchored to procure wood, the water was brackish, and the anchor brought up a mass of putrid leaves, as black as ink. We cut wood in forty-eight hours sufficient to last three months; and found the natives very anxious to trade, either in slaves or ivory.

"'I would recommend no one entering the Congo until the sea breeze sets in strong. The *Fantome,* going 5 knots, was completely turned round two or three times; and great care must be taken to keep on the South shore, as the tide sets directly on the Mona Mazea Bank, and, at such a rapid rate, a ship is almost unmanageable with any wind. In coming down the river (in December we found the water 8 feet deeper than in July), keeping well over on the South shore, we were set directly out of the river. We came down with a 1 knot breeze, the tide running 5 and 6 knots. On the South side of the stream the current appears to set about west by side, *true,* and to the northward of it about *north* by *west, true.*

"'The climate is so fine, that the natives' huts are generally built without roofs. The *Fantome* has been on this station since June; and we have never experienced rain to last one hour, nor any, more than six days, between that time and December 31st, 1840. The thermometer generally in June, July, August, and September, was 70 degrees, and in November and December, 80 degrees to 82 degrees.'"

The new sailing directory for the Ethiopic or southern Atlantic ocean

1857: Waterton, Charles

Charles Waterton; Essays on natural history: 3d series; 2nd edition; Longman, Brown, Green, Longmans, and Roberts; 1857

Charles Waterton writes: "A third ape which has come under my immediate inspection is a young brown chimpanzee, in the Royal

Menagerie of Mrs Wombwell. It was captured on the bank of the river Congo, in Africa."

Essays on natural history: 3d series

1858: Foster, John

John Foster; Henry George Bohn, editor; Fosteriana, consisting of thoughts, reflections, and criticisms, of John Foster: Selected from periodical papers not hitherto published in a collective form; HG Bohn; 1858

John Foster writes: "CONJECTURES RESPECTING CENTRAL AFRICA.

"It can be but slightly conjectured what would have been the fortune of the travellers, who have just terminated their career so far short of their object, had their undertakings been successful. That object, contemplated in prospect, was indeed of a nature to take mighty hold of the imagination, both of those who were to execute the project, and those who were to wait for the result. The greatest part of the ample scene of the enterprise was absolutely unknown, and an unequalled degree of the captivation of mystery was added to this darkness, by the circumstance of a great and renowned river concealing its termination. But it may be permitted to doubt whether the vast region which, in the event of success, would have been for the first time traversed and revealed, would have supplied to us any very enthusiastic gratifications beyond the delight of seeing overcome at last all that had for so many apes defied the investigation. To judge from whatever Park had described and Adams reported, with the addition now of so much as Captain Tuckey was permitted to survey, and all this combined with what we know of many other tracts of Africa, we may be allowed to console ourselves by assuming the probability, that the picture which would have been furnished to us would have been as insignificant as it would have been immense. The determination of the, question respecting the river, would indeed have been a great geographical fact gained. It would have been an exchange of so much ignorance for so much knowledge. Some time or other that knowledge might have become available to some practical utility, as perhaps in the way of commerce; though it is perfectly evident from all that has been seen or reasonably guessed of interior Africa, that ages may pass away before such a state of nature and society can become of any material importance in the economy of European arts and traffic. Meanwhile, on the breaking up and dissipating of the profound and solemn darkness which has for thousands of years rested on this vast, retired, mysterious region, the ardent curiosity which had so long looked towards it in vain, might have sunk in some strange, undefinable sense of disappointment and disenchantment on being permitted to gaze at last on veritable tracts of indifferent earth, and of sand, and of marsh; and on some tribes of miserable barbarians, here thinly spread over a hundred miles of pestilential wilderness, and there more numerously assembled in some *city,* a distant rival of that magnificent far-famed imperial metropolis of golden-roofed palaces and mansions (Timbuctoo), which we have not yet been able to forgive the unlucky stroller Adams for having most innocently happened to discover to be an accumulation of mud huts. It may well be doubted whether, as a mere matter of feeling, this sense of chill and prostration of what had been a fine romantic imaginativeness, would have been compensated by the demonstration of what is so probably the fact, that the river Niger is no other than the river Zaire. So wayward an essence is this spirit of man! - But it is quite time to leave these speculations, and come to the plain official task of giving a brief account of the book before us.

"THE RIVER ZAIRE, CONGO, OR NIGER.

"Till the journey of the intrepid and lamented Park, it was a question for debate, like some theme of the schools, whether a great river, known and famous from ancient times, actually flowed to the west, or to the east. The speculation disposed of thus far, instantly acquired an augmented interest in its latter question - What becomes of the river? After the suggestion of its possibly being, after all, no other than the Nile of Egypt was scientifically set aside, the most plausibility was deemed to attach (perhaps, indeed, because *no* other plausible explanation could be thought of,) to the theory of Major Rennell, that the Niger stops, stagnates, and is evaporated, in some great central lake, north of the line. Nobody, however, cared to let his imagination stop and stagnate there. There was an urgent wish to find this dignified and mysterious stream performing a long ulterior course, and coming out at length from its immense deserts, at some point where we might hail its arrival at the ocean - although we were confounded in attempting to conjecture where so important a point should be to which our extensive knowledge of the African coast had hitherto left us strangers. When, at length, the hitherto little-known river of Congo was described by Mr Maxwell to Park, with a suggestion that *there* might be the object so long sought in vain, he seized the idea with a sanguine eagerness, which soon became a most confident assurance, in spite of the arguments and invincible opinion of so excellent a geographer as Major Rennell."

Fosteriana, consisting of thoughts, reflections, and criticisms, of John Foster: Selected from periodical papers not hitherto published in a collective form

1858: Stone, Elizabeth

Elizabeth Stone; God's acre; or, Historical notices relating to churchyards; 1858

Elizabeth Stone writes: "Among the nations upon the Congo river, a corpse is enveloped in numberless wrappings of cloth, or perhaps of European cotton, the number of which is only limited by the power of the mourner to obtain them - the bulk only restrained with reference to the conveyance to the grave. Accumulating by degrees, this wrapping goes on for years. The larger the bulk, the handsomer is considered the funeral."

God's acre; or, Historical notices relating to churchyards

1859: Great Britain

Great Britain, Lewis Hertslet; A Complete Collection of the Treaties and Conventions, and Reciprocal Regulations at Present Subsisting Between Great Britain and Foreign Powers …: So Far as They Relate to Commerce and Navigation; and to the Repression and Abolition of the Slave Trade; and to the Privileges and Interests of the Subjects of the High Contracting Parties; HM Stationary Office; 1859

Great Britain and Lewis Hertslet write: "(7.) -
Agreement with the Chiefs and Headmen of Congo River.

"June 20, 1854.

"*'Pluto', Congo River, June 20, 1854.*

"BY the express wish of the undersigned Chiefs and Headmen of the Congo River, the following Agreement was entered into, and considered fair and equitable for the mutual protection of trade and commerce between the said Chiefs and Headmen and the British traders.

"ART I. That upon the arrival of any British merchant-vessel in this river for the purpose of trading therein, the Supercargo shall, upon tendering the usual custom to the Chiefs or Headmen entitled to receive it, be allowed the privilege of trading without any further delays or molestation.

"Should the custom not be immediately taken when tendered, the ship is to commence trade; but it does not follow the Supercargo is exempt from paying the custom, if subsequently demanded.

"II. Upon a trader expressing to a Chief or Headman his wish to settle and trade in his territory, he, the said Chief or Headman, shall appoint him a piece of ground to build his factory on; and it is to be distinctly understood by the Chiefs and Headmen, that when the custom is paid or tendered, they, the Chiefs, etc, are responsible for the safety of the lives and property of the traders against their own people, or any others in their territory.

"III. No second custom shall be paid for one voyage of a ship, should it so happen that the Supercargo or Master should die, or should the ship leave to visit other ports, and afterwards return to complete cargo, etc, provided always that it is the same voyage from Europe.

"IV. No Chief or Headman shall, on any pretence whatever, force any trust from any of the British traders, or allow any of his people so to do.

"V. In the event of any misunderstanding between the natives and traders, the Chiefs, Headmen and Masters of the ships shall quietly meet and inquire into the affair; and the Chiefs pledge themselves to punish any offender should he be a native, and the Masters pledge themselves to do the same should he be a white man.

"Should they not then be able to settle the palaver, a letter is to be sent to Her Britannic Majesty's Consul at Loanda, or to one of Her Majesty's ships; but on no such or any other pretence shall the trade be stopped or hindered in any way.

"VI. We, the Chiefs and Headmen of this river, and Masters and Supercargoes of the British vessels, of our own free will, and perfectly understanding the above Articles of this Agreement, consider the same to be perfectly binding to us all, and as a proof thereof, we here, in the presence of Lieutenant-Commander Norman B Bedingfeld, and officers of Her Majesty's ship 'Pluto', affix our names.

"PRINCE MACHILLA. KING MAZELLE. MAMBOOKO DE ZALI. MAFOOKA DE PUNTO. KING MEDORA. MAMBUCO MINGALLI. ZOOAVO LINGUESTER. PRINCE JACK. MANOEL.

"JOHN CHEESEMAN, *Master and Supercargo of the English brig 'Sobraon'.*

"NORMAN B BEDINGFELD, *Lieutenant-Commander HMS 'Pluto'.*

"CAJ HEYSHAM, *Mate HMS 'Pluto'.*

"E SWAIN, *Second Master HMS 'Pluto'.*

"DAVID WILSON, *Assistant Surgeon HMS 'Pluto'.*"

A Complete Collection of the Treaties and Conventions, and Reciprocal Regulations at Present Subsisting Between Great Britain and Foreign Powers...: So ...

1860: Thomas, W

W Thomas; Adventures and observations on the West coast of Africa and its islands, historical and descriptive sketches of Madeira, Canry, Biafra and Cape Verd islands: their climates, inhabitants and productions …; Vol 1; 1860

W Thomas writes: "The Congo River was discovered by Portuguese navigators in the year 1485; and on the banks of its upper waters, and at the foot of the Crystal Mountains they established a trading station, call St Salvador, which has become noted in the history of African trade and slaving. The river, which is six miles wide at its mouth, possesses a good bar, and is navigable to large vessels for several miles, affording safe anchorage. Knowing the people on its banks to be ardent lovers and prosecutors of the slave-trade, the English keep a war steamer constantly cruising about its mouth; but under cover of the American flag, a Yankee clipper goes in occasionally, and watching an opportunity, glides out with a cargo of 'ebony and ivory', alias gentlemen and ladies of color. Sometimes, however, the traitorous winds leave them becalmed on the bar, or they make a mistake in 'guessing' as to the whereabouts of the man-of-war, or an accident befalls them in their flight, and they fall an easy prey to the British Lion. This lion, when he goes to sea, has a voracious appetite for kinky heads and black faces, and when he sees a cargo of them, he will pounce upon them irrespective of the flag that maybe floating overhead. The dependence of the clipper is her heels, and when from light winds, or other causes, these fail her, it not unfrequently happens that, as a *dernier pas,* she discharges her load of human beings into the sea, and escapes while her humane pursuers are trying to rescue the helpless victims of civilized cupidity from the hungry sharks.

"Between the Congo River and the northern boundary of Angola lies the kingdom of Congo, so called, perhaps, for the reason that at some remote period the territory with its many tribes was under the rule of one sovereign. Like Loango, it is at present composed of several independent communities, speaking different languages, but much resembling each other in the form of government and in domestic institutions. The roots of their languages, as well as their physical characteristics, indicate a common origin with the tribes of Loango; which origin has been referred to an extensive family of the plains of the interior. The ethnological relations of the tribes of Africa, particularly of western and central Africa, have been but little studied; and owing to the want of history, the amalgamation of tribes and languages that have taken place by conquest, and the physical changes which have followed migrations from the mountains to the seaboard, or *vice versa,* but little light is to be expected. To philology rather than physiology are we to look for anything useful or satisfactory on this subject."

Adventures and observations on the West coast of Africa and its islands, historical and descriptive sketches of Madeira, Canry, Biafra and Cape Verd islands: …

1861: American Anti-Slavery Society

American Anti-Slavery Society; The anti-slavery history of the John-Brown year: being the twenty-seventh annual report of the American Anti-Slavery Society; 1861

American Anti-Slavery Society writes: "A letter to the New-York *Journal of Commerce,* dated St Helena, Nov 30, mentions a vessel - the Tavernier, 'French built, but evidently fitted out in New York,' - which had just been taken with nearly six hundred Slaves, in a most wretched condition, on board, and names five or six American vessels which had lately escaped the cruisers and left the coast 'with full cargoes'. One of these was 'the bark Rebecca, which *took out some of the emigrants,* of the MCDONOUGH estate, *to Monrovia'* under charter from the Colonization Society, and on her return voyage, had 'gone from the Congo with nine hundred negroes,' - thus doing a double share of 'missionary' work; taking out a cargo of ready-made 'missionaries', and bringing back one of raw material for the manufacture. A letter from Zanzibar, Sept 8, states that 'an American clipper ship took off twelve hundred negroes from the coast a few days since.' In April, of last year, the bark Orion, of New York, was seized in the river Congo, as a suspected Slaver, and sent home for examination; her outfit and internal arrangement being such as to leave scarcely a doubt of her destination, which, moreover, was confessed by her captain, who died on the homeward passage. But, on examination, in June last, she was – *of course,* we might almost say -

released for 'insufficient evidence'; giving another illustration of what the *Journal of Commerce* said, not long ago, that 'the captured Slaver, unless found with his cargo on board, is almost sure to escape in the courts.' On the 30th of November, about five months after her discharge in New York, a British cruiser captured her on the African coast, with nearly nine hundred Slaves on board, - the first mate of the former voyage being now captain, - and surrendered her officers to an American cruiser, to be sent home for trial."

The anti-slavery history of the John-Brown year: being the twenty-seventh annual report of the American Anti-Slavery Society

1862: Stoddard, Elizabeth

Elizabeth Stoddard; The Morgesons; Carleton; 1862

Elizabeth Stoddard writes: "AUNT MERCY had not introduced me to Miss Black as the daughter of Locke Morgeson, the richest man in Surrey, but simply as her neice. Her pride prevented her from making any exhibition of my antecedents, which was wise, considering that I had none. My grandfather, John Morgeson, was a nobody, - merely a 'Co'; and though my great-grandfather, Locke Morgeson, was worthy to be called a Somebody, it was not his destiny to make a stir in the world. Father was a new man. Many of the families of my Barmouth schoolmates had the fulcrum of a monied grandfather. The knowledge of the girls did not extend to that period in the family history when its patriarchs started in the pursuit of Gain. Elmira Sawyer, one of Miss Black's pupils, never heard that her grandfather, 'Black Peter', as he was called, had made excursions, in an earlier part of his life, on the river Congo; or that he was familiar with the soundings of Loango Bay. As he returned from his voyages, bringing more and more money, he enlarged his estate, and grew more and more respectable, retiring at last from the sea, to become a worthy landsman; he paid taxes to church and state, and even had a silver communion cup, among the pewter service used on the occasion of the Lord's Supper; but he never was brought to the approval of that project of the Congregational Churches, - the Colonization of the Blacks to

Liberia. Neither was Hersilia Allen aware that the pink calico in which I first saw her was remotely owing to West India Rum. Nor did Charlotte Alden, the proudest girl in school, know that her grandfather's, Squire Alden's, stepping stone to fortune was the loss of the brig 'Capricorn', which was wrecked in the vicinity of a comfortable port, on her passage out to the whaling ground. An auger had been added to the meagre outfit, and long after the sea had leaked through the hole bored through her bottom, and swallowed her, and the insurance had been paid, the truth leaked out that the captain had received instructions, which had been fulfilled. Whereupon two Insurance Companies went to law with him, and a suit ensued, which ended in their paying costs, in addition to what they had before paid Squire Alden, who winked in a derisive manner at the Board of Directors, when he received its check."

The Morgesons

1863: Hunt, James

James Hunt; On the Negro's Place in Nature; Trubner, for the Anthropological Society; 1863

James Hunt writes: "In the first place, I would explain that I understand by Negro, the dark, woolly-headed African found in the neighbourhood of the Congo river. Africa contains, like every other continent, a large number of different races, and these have become very much mixed. These races may be estimated as a whole at about 150 millions, occupying a territory of between 13 and 14 millions of square miles. I shall not enter into any disquisition as to the great diversity of physical conformation that is found in different races, but shall simply say that my remarks will be confined to the typical woolly-headed Negro. Not only is there a large amount of mixed blood in Africa, but there are also apparently races of very different physical characters, and in as far as they approach the typical Negro, so far will my remarks apply to them. But I shall exclude entirely from consideration all those who have European, Asiatic, Moorish or Berber blood in their veins."

On the Negro's place in nature

1865: Christie, William Dougal

William Dougal Christie; Notes on Brazilian Questions; Macmillan and Co; 1865

William Dougal Christie writes: "'At the same time, I imagine that your Excellency will coincide with myself in thinking it a remarkable circumstance that, almost at the period when your Excellency, in Rio, was demanding, not rumours, but the legal conviction of the complicity of this Sa in the slave-trade, the Imperial steamer 'Urania' should have captured at Itabapoama, a slave-vessel with 400 Africans on board, belonging notoriously to this slave-dealer Sa, whose cashier, one Antonio Sevelino de Avellar, a well-known slave-dealer of the River Zaire, was on the spot, waiting to receive these unhappy victims of this ennobled kidnapper."

Notes on Brazilian questions

1869: Timbs, John

John Timbs; Eccentricities of the Animal Creation; Seeley, Jackson and Halliday; 1869

John Timbs writes: "Professor Smith and Captain Tuckey, in exploring the Congo River, in South Africa, saw in a beautiful sandy cove, at the opening of a creek, behind a long projecting point, an immense number of Hippopotami; and in the evening a number of alligators were also seen there; an association hardly consistent with the hostility related by Hasselquist."

Eccentricities of the animal creation

1871: Hawkey, Charlotte

Charlotte Hawkey; Neota; privately printed for Mrs Charlotte Hawkey; 1871

Charlotte Hawkey writes: "A congeniality in their tastes and pursuits had laid the foundation of a firm friendship between my brother and Lieutenant Tuckey, RN, who had suffered under almost as long a detention as himself, and with similar assiduity had devoted his attention to such professional subjects as it was possible under such circumstances to study with advantage. The results of his application appeared on his return to England, when he published his valuable work on 'Maritime Geography', in four volumes, and after receiving the merited reward of promotion to the rank of commander, was appointed by the Admiralty to the command of an expedition which it had been determined to send to the south of Africa, to explore the river Zaire, or Congo. Captain Tuckey was permitted to select his own officers (who were all volunteers), and he immediately offered my brother, his former companion in captivity, the post of lieutenant, only one officer of that rank being to accompany the expedition. The offer was at once accepted by Lieutenant Hawkey, who resigned his appointment to the 'Cyrus' sloop-of-war, in which he was serving at the time, and under the date of October 27, 1815, wrote to me as follows: -

"'M- has told you, no doubt, all about the Congo expedition I am about to embark in. It is a hazardous but very interesting undertaking, as the interior of Africa is very little known to Europeans, and we shall take out scientific men, that all the information possible in the different branches of natural history, botany, and comparative anatomy may be collected. We have a native of a kingdom called Betandee to accompany us; he will be left in his native country if he wishes it, seven or eight hundred miles up the Congo, which by some is supposed to be the embouchure of the Niger, by others to have its source on the eastern side of Africa, but that we are to decide if possible. So much for the nature of the voyage; and no more until I see you, which will be now very soon, I hope. I am very much obliged to you and M- for your kindness in assisting me to fit out. Go on and prosper; if your work is good I will show it to the Emperor of Timbuctoo, and tell him a European princess wrought it me.'"

Neota

1872: Burton, Sir Richard Francis

Sir Richard Francis Burton; Zanzibar: City, Island, and Coast; Vol 2; Tinsley brothers; 1872

Sir Richard Francis Burton writes: "Nothing even among the Somali Bedawin can be wilder than the specimens from Ukamba-ni; these Warimangao,* as the people of Mombasah call them, the 'sons' of the chief Kivoi, that danced and sang the Nyunbo or song of triumph in the streets of Mombasah. It was a perfect picture of savagery. About 50 blacks, ruddled with ochre, performed the Zumo (procession); men blowing Kudu-horns, or firing their muskets, and women 'lullalooing'. They sat with us for some hours drinking a sherbet of Ngizi, or molasses extracted from cocoa-tree toddy, and the number of gallons which disappeared were a caution. The warriors of the tribe, adorned with beads on the necks, loins, and ankles, were armed with the usual long bows and poisoned arrows, spears or rather javelins, knobsticks for striking or throwing; knives and two-edged swords of fine iron, the latter a rude imitation of the straight Omani blade, of which I afterwards saw specimens upon the Congo river. Some had shock heads of buttered hair, wondrous unsavoury, and fit only for door-mats; others wore the thatch twisted into a hundred little corkscrews; their eyes were wild and staring, their voices loud and barking, and all their gestures denoted the 'noble savage' who had run out of his woods for the first time. They were, however, in high spirits. Before last year (1857) no Arab had visited their country: trading parties from Ukamba-ni sold ivory to the Wanyika for four times round the tusk in beads, and these middlemen, after fleecing those more savage than themselves, retailed the goods at high profits to the citizens. The Wakamba of the coast are, of course, anxious to promote intercourse between Mombasah and their kinsmen of the interior, and thus the road, first opened at the imminent risk of life, by the enterprising Dr Krapf, has become a temporary highway into the interior of Eastern Intertropical Africa - a region abounding in varied interest, and still awaiting European exploration. But let not geographers indulge in golden visions of the future! Some day the Arabs of Mombasah will seize and sell a caravan, or the fierce Wamasai or the Gallas will prevail against the traders. Briefly, no spirit of prophecy is needed to foresee that the Kikuyu line shall share the fate of many others.

"*The singular is Mrimangao, hence MrCooley's Meremongao, whence iron was exported to make Damascus blades - risum teneatis? Dr Krapf says 'the Wakamba are called by the Suahili, Waumanguo. M Guillain (iii 216) translates 'M'rimanggao, or Ouarimanggao' by 'gens qui vont nus.'"

Sir Richard Francis Burton continues: "The men chip their teeth to points, and, like the Wasumbara, punch out in childhood one incisor from the lower jaw; a piece of dried rush or sugar-cane distends the ear-lobe to an unsightly size. All carried bows and arrows. Some shouldered such hoes and hatchets as English children use upon the sands: here bounteous earth, fertilized by the rains of heaven, requires merely the scratching of a man's staff. Others led stunted curs, much like the pariah dogs of Hindostan, adorned with leather collars: I afterwards saw similar pets at the Yellalah of the Congo river. The animals are prime favourites with the savages, as were the Spanish puppies in the days of Charles II; they hold a dog-stew to be a dish fit for a king. In West Africa also the meat finds many admirers, and some missionaries in the Niger regions have described it as somewhat glutinous, but 'very sweet'. Why should we not have cynophages as well as hippophages?"

Sir Richard Francis Burton continues: "We followed the Arab line of traffic, first laid open to Lake Tanganyika by Sayf bin Said el Muameri, about 1825. The existence of a beaten path in Africa has its advantages and its disadvantages. The natives are accustomed to travellers; they no longer perpetually attribute to them supernatural and pernicious powers, nor do they, except amongst the worst tribes, expect every manner of evil to follow the portent: it is not difficult to engage hands, nor is it impossible to collect information concerning regions which cannot be visited. At the same time, contact with the slave-dealer has increased cupidity and has diminished hospitality: the African loses all sense of savage honour, without learning to replace it by commercial honesty, and all his ingenuity is devoted to the contrivance and the carrying out of 'avanies'. But where, on the other hand, the explorer must hew his own way - such was the case with Paul du Chaillu from the Gaboon region, and with myself up the Congo river - and where there is no prescriptive right of transit even for pay, the adventure waxes far more difficult and dangerous. Here we see the African at home, an unmitigated savage, unmodified by acquaintance with the outer world, dwelling in the presence of his brethren, and rich in all the contrarieties of the racial character. His suspicions and his desires are at once aroused. His horror of new things struggles with his wish to make the most of them; he has no precedent for his demands, and consequently he has no sense of their absurdity. A caravan is to him a 'Doummoulafong', or thing sent to be eaten, as Mungo Park's second expedition was called. A Portuguese officer has been asked 120 dollars by the Wamakua for permission to visit a hill behind Mozambique, distant some 25 miles from the sea. At the Yellalah, or Rapids of the Congo river, I was required to pay, before leave to advance could be given, a fee in goods which would have amounted to 200 pounds. And expense is not the main obstacle to the success of these exceptional expeditions: the merest accident with a fire-arm may render progress impossible, and may endanger the lives of the whole party."

Zanzibar: City, island, and coast

1873: The Lands of Cazembe

The Lands of Cazembe: Lacerda's Journey to Cazembe in 1798; Murray; 1873

The Lands of Cazembe writes: "The above declares that, when sent by the Mambo Cazembe his master to the Kinglet (regulo) Muropoe,* during three months' march, he crossed in small canoes four streams like this (southern) Zambeze. The first was the Roapura,** the second was the Mufira,*** the third was the Guarava,**** and the fourth was the Rofoi.***** In this distance, where the land belongs to the Varunda nation,****** there are but four settlements, one on each river; and the people live on milho burro, maize (Zea Mays) and manioc. From the lands of the Maropoe to those of the Mueneputo (a chief so called from the Portuguese), either on the east or on the west, it is one month's journey, and whites (Muzengos)******* come up with their slaves to purchase ivory and captives. The sea is large and salt, and from the sun-dried water they derive the salt brought for their Mambo.******** On the other side of this sea-arm also appear large masted vessels, and houses as big as ours. The further bank of the river (Zaire or Congo) is occupied by the Congo kinglet,********* a neighbour of the whites. Whatever cloth he receives from them annually he divides with the said Mueneputo and the Muropoe.

"*This is the usual African style of exalting the master at the expense of truth.

"**This stream has been before alluded to, under the name of Luapula. It was found by Dr Livingstone to connect the Bangweolo, or Bemba, with the Moore Lake.

"***All African rivers have half-a-dozen names. We must, therefore, not be surprised if we do not find these words in other travels. The only check upon this march is that made by the two Pombeiros, sent in 1802 by Sr Francisco Honorato da Costa. The Mufira, alias Rufira, Luvira, or 'Luvivi', is a stream 12 fathoms wide, and laid down as an affluent of the Ruapura or Luapula, crossed by Pedro Joao Baptista on the 55th day. According to Mr Cooley, it is the great river Luviri, called by the Arabs Lufira, which flows into the Luapula about 100 miles southwest or south-southwest from the City of the Cazembe. Dr Livingstone first throws it into the Tanganyika Lake: he now makes it rise, under the name of Luviri, on the western watershed of Conda Irugo, to the south of which is Lake Bangweolo: it thus takes the name of Lufira (Bartle Frere's 'Lualaba') and falls into Lake Ulenge, or Kamalondo.

"****This Guarava is evidently an influent of the great Lulua, or Lualaba, a stream 50 fathoms wide, and formerly laid down as one of the head waters of the Leeambye or Upper Zambeze. It was crossed by Pedro on the 41st day of his march, and he found a large settlement there.

"*****The Rofoi must be another eastern feeder of the Great Lulua or Lualaba. We find in Dr Livingstone's last labours a Ropoeji influent, crossed by the Pombeiros.

"******Pedro calls these people Viajantes Arundas and Viajantes da Alundas. Bowdich terms them the nation of the Varoondas. Mr Cooley, with extreme error, explains, by the Congo languages, Alunda or Arunda - elsewhere he tells us that the Alunda never pronounce the letter R - to mean mountaineers or bushmen. It is clearly Alunda, Balunda, or Walunda, according to dialect, the great nation ruled over by the Muata ya Nvo: hence Lunda (Mr Cooley's Roonda), the oily of the Cazembe. (See Dr Livingstone's first map.)

"********Muzungo is the Mundele, or Mondele, of the Congo, hence Dr Livingstone's 'Babindele, or Portuguese' ('First Expedition', chap xix). That traveller uses 'Bazunga' for Portuguese, and mistakes it for 'half-castes'; whilst he calls Englishmen Makoa (sing Lekoa). Muzungu is the general East African name for a white man, Uzungu being the land of the white man. Mr Cooley ('Inner Africa Laid Open', p 35) explains Muzungu to mean 'properly, wise men': at Zanzibar I have heard this derivation. Dr Livingstone ('Second Expedition', xvi p 331) takes it from 'zunga', to visit or wander, perhaps a little too fanciful.

"*********Many African tribes (*eg,* the Bube of Fernando Po) hold salt to be a bad substitute for salt water. I have seen sea-water drunk even in the Cape Verde Islands.

"**********The great and powerful Manicongo (Lord of Congo) was certainly not tributary to the Muropue; nor have his smaller successors ever been dependent upon the latter."

The Lands of Cazembe: Lacerda's Journey to Cazembe in 1798

1874: Hoppin, James Mason

James Mason Hoppin; Life of Andrew Hull Foote, Rear-admiral United States Navy: With a Portrait and Illustrations; American culture series; Library of American civilization; Harper; 1874

James Mason Hoppin writes: "On the 8th of January, 1851, the Perry again reported herself to the commander-in-chief at Porto Praya, after one year's service on the African coast. Here she made preparations for a third southern cruise. As the slave-trade had been pretty much driven out of Ambriz, and had shifted itself to the Congo River, the Perry proceeded thither, encountering on the passage a heavy tornado. Lieutenant Foote thus describes the Congo River:

"'The river is more than two leagues broad at its mouth. At the distance of eight or ten miles seaward, in a northeasterly direction, the water preserves its freshness; and at the distance of fifty and even sixty miles it has a black tinge. Here are often seen small islands floating seaward, formed of fibrous roots, bamboo, rushes, and long grass, and covered with birds. The banks of the Congo are lined with low mangrove bushes, with clumps of a taller species interspersed, growing to the height of seventy feet. Palm-trees, and other trees of a smaller growth, are seen with a rich and beautiful foliage. In going up the river, the southern shore should be hugged, where there is plenty of water close to the land. The current is so strong - often running six miles an hour off Shark's Point - that an exceedingly fresh sea-breeze is necessary in order to stem the stream. The greatest strength of this current, however, is superficial, not extending more than six or eight feet in depth. The Congo, like all the rivers of Africa, except the Nile, is navigable but a short distance before reaching the rapids. The great central region being probably not less than three thousand feet in altitude above the sea, these rapids are formed by a sudden depression of the surface of the country toward the sea, or by a bed of hard rock stretching across the basin of the river.'

"A paper of considerable hydrographical interest in relation to the Congo River and the navigation of the southern equatorial coast of Africa was drawn up by the first lieutenant of the ship, Mr Porter, and, after having been carefully supervised by the commander, was dispatched to the United States National Observatory, and has since been published in 'Maury's Sailing Directions'."

Life of Andrew Hull Foote, Rear-admiral United States Navy: With a Portrait and Illustrations

1874: Staden, Hans

Hans Staden; Sir Richard Francis Burton, editor; Albert Tootal, translator; The Captivity of Hans Stade in Hesse: In AD 1547-1555, Among the Wild Tribes of Eastern Brazil; Vol 51; Issue 51 of Hakluyt Society works, first series; Hakluyt Society; 1874

Hans Staden writes: "After walking a league I reached the Bairro de S Francisco, one of those small outlying places which astonish the traveller in the Brazil. In a village with a single street of scattered houses, backed by cocoa-nuts and large clearings, and fronted by a Praia (beach) bearing a few canoes, rises a vast and lofty building of the best masonry, approached by a fine ramp of masonry, and faced by a substantial stone cross. To the north is a chapel of the Third Order of Franciscans, now a Matriz: in the centre and fronting east is the convent church, with a portico supported by two piers and flanked by a tower. The southern building is a huge convent, which once accommodated a score of monks, and might have lodged a hundred. Azulejos (Lisbon glazed tiles) upon the tower, the dome and the facade, prove that no expense was spared: both places of worship show St Francis and his stigmata, whilst both have black St Benedicts in gorgeous array, each holding a white baby.* But everything is in the last stage of neglect; the kitchen, with the vast chimney, looks utterly deserted; the cloisters are falling to pieces; the floors are dangerous, and the torn music-scores are scattered on the ground - I saw something of the kind on the Congo River. Tradition says that the land was given by an old 'Morador; (colonist), Antonio de Abreu, and doubtless a whole regiment of slaves, and probably of Indians, was employed upon the construction. It belongs to careless owners in Rio de Janeiro; the difficulty is to know what to do with it, were it even secularised. The Freguezia (parish) is one of the most populous in the Province, but men have changed their habitations, and there are no monks to be lodged. At the Bairro, antimony was ignored by all the inhabitants.

"*One morning I awoke and actually found a black Benedict in a most peculiar costume, placed right above my head. The white Saint Benedict in these regions is called Sao Bento."

The Captivity of Hans Stade of Hesse: In AD 1547-1555, Among the Wild Tribes of Eastern Brazil

1875: Jones, Charles H

Charles H Jones; Africa: The History of Exploration and Adventure as Given in the Leading Authorities from Herodotus to Livingstone; H Holt; 1875

Charles H Jones writes: "To the south of this region, Africa is a great mass of elevated land, rising more or less above the level of the sea. Some geographers have maintained that they can trace a system of terraces on all sides. It is certainly so on the southern side, but the same feature is not discernible throughout. Indeed, generally speaking, the plateau on the other sides either gradually slopes down into a plain along the sea-shore, or rises abruptly out of the sea, and presents a deep edge of from seven thousand to eight thousand feet elevation. The edge of the table-land is, however, usually from one hundred to three hundred miles distant from the sea. Beginning at Cape Colony, there is an almost uninterrupted table-land, extending to the north for at least one thousand geographical miles. The basin of the Orange River forms the southern portion, and this is succeeded by the Kalahari Desert, which is again continued by the basin of the Sesheke and Lake Ngami, there being many rivers, while the whole region is level, and Ngami two thousand eight hundred and twenty-five feet above the sea. There is no doubt a connection between this territory and the basin of the Zambesi. To the north, the ground rises and forms the water-shed between the basins of the Congo River and Lake Nyassa. In this region were supposed to lie 'the Mountains of the Moon', so frequently mentioned in the ancient geography of Africa. The site of them was continually shifted from one latitude to another, while all agreed that they ran from east to west; but Dr Beke, from personal observation, determined that they had a direction from south to north, and were parallel with the eastern coast, and that they form the southern continuation of the Abyssinian table-land. The most elevated peaks rise on the outer edge of the range, between it and the coast, and as isolated cones. The Kenia and Kilimanjaro, part of this system, and two of its peaks, are, as we have said, snowy mountains, and, that being their character, they must have an elevation of at least twenty thousand feet. Abba Yared, in the northern edge of the Abyssinian table-land, is fifteen thousand feet; Mendif, south of Lake Tsad, is isolated, and is probably ten thousand feet high; and Alautika, conspicuous to the south of Yola, 8 degrees 30 minutes north latitude, 13 degrees 45 minutes East longotide, is also isolated, and estimated by Dr Barth at ten thousand. The loftiest of the Cameroons is thirteen thousand seven hundred and sixty feet high, and, in Southern Africa, the Spits Kop, or Compass Berg, is ten thousand two hundred and fifty."

Charles H Jones continues: "The British colony of Sierra Leone extends from Rokelle River in the north, to Eater River in the south, and reaches about twenty miles inland. The Malaghetta or Grain Coast extends from Sierra Leone to Cape Palmas. It is sometimes styled the Windy or Windward Coast. The Republic of Liberia occupies a considerable extent of this country, and among the population are many liberated slaves, freed in former times in the United States. The Ivory Coast extends from Cape Palmas to Cape Three Points, and obtained its name from the quantity of ivory supplied by the numerous elephants to be found there. The Gold Coast stretches from Cape Three Points to the River Volta, and has been long frequented for gold-dust and other products. The Slave Coast extends from the River Volta to the Calabar River, and was formerly the scene of an immense slave traffic. The kingdoms of Ashanti, Dahomey, and others, occupy the interior country of the Guinea Coast. The coast from Old Calabar River to the Portuguese possessions is inhabited by various tribes. Duke's Town, on the former river, is a large town of thirty thousand to forty thousand inhabitants. Loango extends from the equator to the Zaire, or Congo, River. Congo extends south of the Zaire, and is very fertile, with veins of copper and iron. Angola includes the two districts of Angola proper and Benguela. Here the Portuguese settlements reach farther inland than in the preceding districts, namely, two hundred miles. The population of these settlements is about four hundred thousand, including about two thousand Europeans. The Capital, St Paolo de Loando, has one thousand six hundred European and four thousand native inhabitants. There is a fine harbor."

Charles H Jones continues: "Captain Tuckey, as we have already seen, commanded an English expedition for exploring the Congo River, which made the attempt in 1816, without accomplishing much in the way of discovery. Captain Bedingfield organized a fresh expedition in 1864. There was no difficulty in ascending the river for upwards of one hundred miles; but at that point there are formidable rapids through which the stream rushes between high rocks. These form a great impediment to navigation; but beyond them, for the 180 miles of its course which have been explored, the Congo is again a noble stream, maintaining a width of from one to five miles. Its source is unknown, but the German geographer Petermann regards it as identical with Livingstone's Lualaba, and hence as connected with the vast lacustrine system of the equatorial region. Further explorations are now (October, 1874) in progress, which it is to be hoped will settle this latter question."

Charles H Jones continues: "JAMES KINGSTON TUCKEY was born in 1778, at Greenhill, in the county of Cork, Ireland. He entered the navy at an early age, went to India in 1794, was employed in surveying the coast of New South Wales, was taken prisoner by the French in 1805, and remained in captivity till 1814. He was then selected to command the expedition for exploring the River Congo, and died in Africa, in 1816. He was the author of 'Maritime Geography and Statistics', in four volumes, written during his imprisonment, besides narratives of his voyages to Australia and Congo."

Africa: The History of Exploration and Adventure as Given in the Leading Authorities from Herodotus to Livingstone

Coming soon...

Interesting History of Saturn

Already published:

INTERESTING PLACE NAMES AND HISTORY SERIES:

Interesting Place Names and History of America

Revised Interesting Place Names and History of Australia

Interesting Place Names and History of Canada

Interesting Place Names and History of England

Revised Interesting Place Names and History of Ireland

Interesting Place Names and History of New Zealand

Interesting Place Names and History of Northern Ireland

Interesting Place Names and History of Scotland

Interesting Place Names and History of South Africa

Interesting Place Names and History of Wales

***TRAGIC* (BUT INTERESTING) HISTORY SERIES:**

Tragic (but Interesting) History of Anti-Semitism and Persecution of Jews

INTERESTING HISTORY OF RANDOM PHENOMENA SERIES:

Interesting History of Tsunamis and Big Waves

INTERESTING HISTORY OF RIVERS SERIES:

Interesting History of the Columbia River

Interesting History of the Saint Lawrence River

Interesting History of the Zambezi River

INTERESTING HISTORY OF LAKES SERIES:

Interesting History of Lake Superior

INTERESTING HISTORY OF COASTAL CITIES SERIES:

Interesting History of Baltimore [Maryland, USA]

Interesting History of Kolkata aka Calcutta

Interesting History of Lagos [Nigeria]

INTERESTING HISTORY OF FOLKLORE SERIES:

Interesting History of "Bad" Poetry

Interesting History of Giants

Interesting History of Stonehenge

MEMOIRS:

This Dark Earth (published under scribd.com by Emily Stehr; published under amazon.com by Amelia Jones)

Knife Allergy and Treatment Plan: How I Didn't Cut My Throat, But I Did Cut My Forearm; My Journey Through Combat, Suicide, and Self-Harm

Printed in Great Britain
by Amazon